MARCO  POLO

LANZAROTE

ATLANTIC
OCEAN **PORTUGAL**
Azores (Port.)   Cádiz

                                    MOROCCO

Madeira (Port.)

Canary Islands
(Spain)   **Lanzarote**

                        Western
                        Sahara

D0321635

The best Insider Tips → p. 4

INSIDER TIP

Best of... → p. 6

Arrecife → p. 32

Costa Teguise/North → p. 40

SYMBOLS

INSIDER TIP   Insider Tip
★   Highlight
● ● ● ●   Best of ...
☼   Scenic view
😊   Responsible travel: for ecological or fair trade aspects
(*)   Telephone numbers that are not toll-free

PRICE CATEGORIES HOTELS

Expensive	over 150 euros
Moderate	70–150 euros
Budget	under 70 euros

Prices for a double room, for two persons per night with breakfast (in a hotel); without breakfast (in an apartment)

PRICE CATEGORIES RESTAURANTS

Expensive	over 20 euros
Moderate	10–20 euros
Budget	under 10 euros

Prices for a meal with starter and main course (no drinks)

On the cover: Vines, pretty villages and beautiful beaches p.60 | A visit to little sister p. 49

CONTENTS

P. d. Carmen/Centre → p. 60

Timanfaya NP → p. 72

Playa Blanca/South → p. 76

Road atlas → p. 118

MAPS IN THE GUIDEBOOK
(120 A1) Page numbers and coordinates refer to the road atlas.
(0) Site/address located off the map. Coordinates are also given for places that are not marked on the road atlas. Maps for Arrecife and Puerto del Carmen can be found inside the back cover

INSIDE BACK COVER:
PULL-OUT MAP →

PULL-OUT MAP 🔲
(🔲 A–B 2–3) Refers to the removable pull-out map

The best MARCO POLO Insider Tips

Our top 15 Insider Tips

INSIDER TIP ▶ Heavenly drinks

Star's City serves up not just a stunning view, but also great cocktails. At night there's a sensational view from what is the highest building on the island, but it's just as good during the day when the eye is drawn to wave-battered reefs, beaches and the southern peninsula → p. 37

INSIDER TIP ▶ Martial arts Lanzarotean style

You have just got to be there as the tension mounts among wrestlers and spectators at a lucha canaria contest → p. 23

INSIDER TIP ▶ At one with the Snow Virgin

Climb to the Ermita de las Nieves, a hermitage dedicated to the Our Lady of the Snows, and you will enjoy what is surely the most spectacular view of the island, plus thunderous sound effects from the pounding surf → p. 57

INSIDER TIP ▶ In the house of Omar Sharif

The charismatic actor lost this extraordinary property in a high-stakes game of bridge. Luckily, you can now take a stroll through the halls and the labyrinth of passages in the rock at LagOmar → p. 58

INSIDER TIP ▶ In the old harbour

If you are looking for a quiet and intimate setting in a delightful spot against the maritime backdrop of Puerto del Carmen, and want to enjoy a fine meal at the same time, then the Casa Roja restaurant is the perfect place → p. 64

INSIDER TIP ▶ Like a mirage

In the evening the dromedaries make their way back to the stables from the land of the pitch-black Timanfaya Mountains. A surreal sight, it could almost be a mirage (photo above) → p. 21

INSIDER TIP ▶ Fish supper at sunset

The fishing village of El Golfo (photo right) is always worth a detour, particularly at sunset, when the fire-red sun on the horizon sinks into the sea to the sound of screeching seagulls. The

Bogavante restaurant boasts not just a menu of delicious seafood, but also an extraordinary ambience → **p. 84**

INSIDER TIP Partying by the sea

The DJs at Biosfera in Arrecife stoke up a torrid atmosphere beneath a giant awning that opens out onto the promenade. So it never gets too crowded here → **p. 38**

INSIDER TIP Underground music

The lava caves at the Cueva de los Verdes rank among Lanzarote's highlights. Even more impressive is a visit to the caves for one of the rare concerts in the auditorium → **p. 102**

INSIDER TIP Wine from the fiery earth

The wine-makers at the Bodega Stratvs have had to work hard to nurture these delicate vines. Drop in for a tasting and judge for yourself how successful they've been → **p. 68**

INSIDER TIP Dine out with Orlando

It's mainly locals who eat here. At Lilium in Arrecife, almost all of the ingredients are sourced on the island; the formula is fusion and the decor hip. Señor Orlando serves Lanzarote's best wines → **p. 37**

INSIDER TIP True island fashion

Ladies' fashions, mainly in linen but also in other materials, form the basis of the collections by Romy B in Playa Blanca – exciting clothes and accessories made in Lanzarote → **p. 80**

INSIDER TIP Market madness

At the weekend mercadillos specialising in crafts and farmhouse products and produce pop up everywhere. Probably the Saturday market in Haría has the liveliest atmosphere → **p. 57**

INSIDER TIP It feels like a private villa

As soon as you enter Villa Vik, you will feel at ease. There are only 14 rooms, but even so it boasts spacious lounges, tranquil terraces and a pool in the garden → **p. 39**

INSIDER TIP Cuba meets the Canary Islands

Musicians flock to the Os Gallegos restaurant on Sunday to eat with Señor Antonio and to play samba and salsa. Good music and good seafood! → **p. 48**

BEST OF ...

FOR FREE

● *Sunbathe in powder sand*

They are well away from all the tourist commotion, get few visitors and are not at all commercialised. Near *Órzola* in the far north is a series of several bays, where the snow-white sand contrasts beautifully with the tar-black rock. A lovely spot for a picnic → p. 48

● *For the sure-footed*

There is normally an admission charge to see César Manrique's land-scape artworks, such as the Mirador del Río (photo), the viewing platform over the straits between Lanzarote and the neighbouring island of La Graciosa. Just as spectacular, but free, is the view from the *Mirador de Guinate*, and, what's more, it's quite likely that you will have the place to yourself → p. 58

● *A lesson in vulcanology*

Viewed from outside the *Visitor Centre* at Timanfaya National Park juxtaposes the traditional and the modern. What is impressive about the inside is the fascinating multi-media introduction to the geology of volcanoes → p. 75

● *Sunbathe in comfort*

The beaches in *Puerto del Carmen* are very pretty and very popular. If you'd like to bask in the sun in greater comfort, then you have to pay for a lounger. But after 5pm all the beach furniture is free – and there will still be another two hours of sun to enjoy → p. 65

● *A walk with a view*

You can save yourself the car-parking charge for the nature conservation area if you walk from the seaside promenade at Playa Blanca to the *Papagayo beaches*. And there's an added bonus: magnificent views over to Fuerteventura. → p. 85

● *To the heart of darkness*

Employees of *Timanfaya National Park* take visitors where others can't go. The tour on foot explores craters, tunnels and an almost level, solid sea of lava in the middle of the Fire Mountains → p. 74

●●●●● Dots in guidebook refer to 'Best of ...' tips

● *Wine from a volcano*

The malvasia grape produces wines in a number of varieties ranging from very dry to very sweet. Vines grow in lava pits, where moisture from the night-time dew collects. The accumulated water is then released to the vine roots during the course of the day. Miraculously, Lanzarote's stony wasteland becomes a fertile vineyard, and the wines from *El Chupadero* prove it (photo) → **p. 68**

● *Journey back in time*

Nowhere else is Lanzarote's past more evident than in *Teguise*. In the *real villa*, the royal town, fine mansions and elegant town houses, narrow alleys, broad plazas and dignified churches gloriously reveal the island's history → **p. 52**

● *Salt from sun and sea*

Nothing imparts a more intensive taste to our food than *sal del mar* or sea salt. This white gold is harvested in the *Salinas de Janubio* and you can purchase it at low prices in the Mirador Salinas restaurant → **p. 85**

● *Old sounds, new timples*

The timple arrived on the island with the African slaves, its bright sound an essential part of the Lanzarotean folk song. This small stringed instrument is crafted by hand in *Teguise in small workshops*, such as the one run by Antonio Lemes Hernández → **p. 56**

● *Beauty from the bowels of the earth*

If you are taking a stroll on one of Lanzarote's lava-strewn beaches, be on the look-out, as you may come across a piece of olivine: a semi-precious, translucent olive-green gemstone, which looks at its best set in silver → **p. 85**

● *To wolf island*

Tours to the nature reserve of Isla de Lobos leave from Playa Blanca. The island used to be a habitat for the sea wolf, also known as the monk seal *(lobo marinero)*, now one of Europe's most endangered mammals. Sadly, they have been extinct on the island for many years. Of interest now are the volcanic *hornitos*, patches of sand covered entirely by shells, and a lighthouse → **p. 80**

● *Forgotten recipes*

There are still chefs around who love to prepare traditional dishes using ingredients sourced on the island. Two good exponents of this dying art are the *Isla Bonita* in Costa Teguise and the Casa del Campesino in Mozaga → **p. 43, 69**

ONLY IN

BEST OF ...

● Stark contrasts

The sturdy *Castillo de San José*, high above the harbour at Arrecife, is paradoxically the stunning venue for displays of contemporary art. The brightly coloured paintings displayed in the dark barrel vaults reflect the work of a generation of Canarian artists, mainly from the 1950s to the 1970s → p. 35

● Where the power lay

See for yourself what life was like for an aristocratic family living on Lanzarote in the 18th and 19th centuries. Explore this grand mansion and you will gain a fascinating insight into what power and wealth meant to the island's elite in the *Palacio de Spínola* in Teguise → p. 55

● Dive deep

It's not just children who will enjoy the Submarine Safari and fascinating glimpses of marine life at a depth of 30m from the window of a bright yellow vessel. Excursions start from Puerto del Carmen and Puerto Calero (photo) → p. 70, 80

● Lazy days over coffee and cakes

The *Café La Unión* in Arrecife is a delightful spot to while away the day, if you cannot get to the beach. Follow that with a viewing of the artworks in the Sala José Saramago opposite → p. 36

● An emotional roller coaster

You will need several hours to sample the many stations in the Roman-inspired bathing complex at the *Iberostar Costa Calero:* saltwater, seawater, heated pools, music pools, various saunas, plus the warm thalasso spa bath with massage. In the form of a wild river the pool flows out into the lava garden → p. 70

● Eye to eye with a shark

A 2 metre-long nurse shark and Conan, a 1.50 m sting ray, patrol the large tank at Lanzarote Aquarium *in Costa Teguise. B*rave souls can go swimming with the sharks and other predators, but always in the company of a diving instructor and a biologist → p. 100

RAIN

RELAX AND CHILL OUT
Take it easy and spoil yourself

● *Sit and watch the hang gliders*

Sit in the *Chiringo Beach* bar overlooking the sand with tapas and a cool beer and admire the skills of the hang-glider pilots as they come into land on the Playa de Arrieta – quite a spectacle and so easy to enjoy → **p. 46**

● *Where the Canary Islands stop*

Walk along the *Playa de las Conchas*, the 'shell beach' at the north end of La Graciosa, then stop to watch wave after wave crashing against the shoreline and the scattering of rocky outcrops. Make the most of Lanzarote's much smaller northern neighbour → **p. 49**

● *The first bar in town*

When mariners arrive at the Marina Rubicón in Playa Blanca, they have to pass *Bar One,* outstanding in more ways than one. Nowhere else will you sense the yearning for the open sea more than here → **p. 79**

● *In harmony with the elements*

Volcanic earth for beauty treatments and sea salt from the island for peelings, seaweed wraps and moisturising aloe vera: the miraculous healing power of nature is deployed in the *spa zone at the Princesa Yaiza* Suite Hotel → **p. 16**

● *Out at sea*

The wind blows and the waves crash out at sea. But if you are watching the underwater world pass by from the glass bottom of the *Princesa Icó catamaran,* it's much, much calmer → **p. 65**

● *The perfect place to chill out*

The home of chill-out music is Ibiza, but go to the Canary Island branch of the *Café del Mar* in Playa Blanca and you will hear the same laid-back sounds, here amid the ultra-cool setting of pastel shades and silver → **p. 79**

● *Once a hermit's house*

For many years, Hilario Lanzaroteño, a soldier who later adopted a hermit lifestyle, lived on the outskirts of Yaiza. His estate, restored by an eccentric art-lover, is now an exclusive country hotel and the perfect refuge for those in search of peace and tranquillity (photo) → **p. 87**

INTRODUCTION

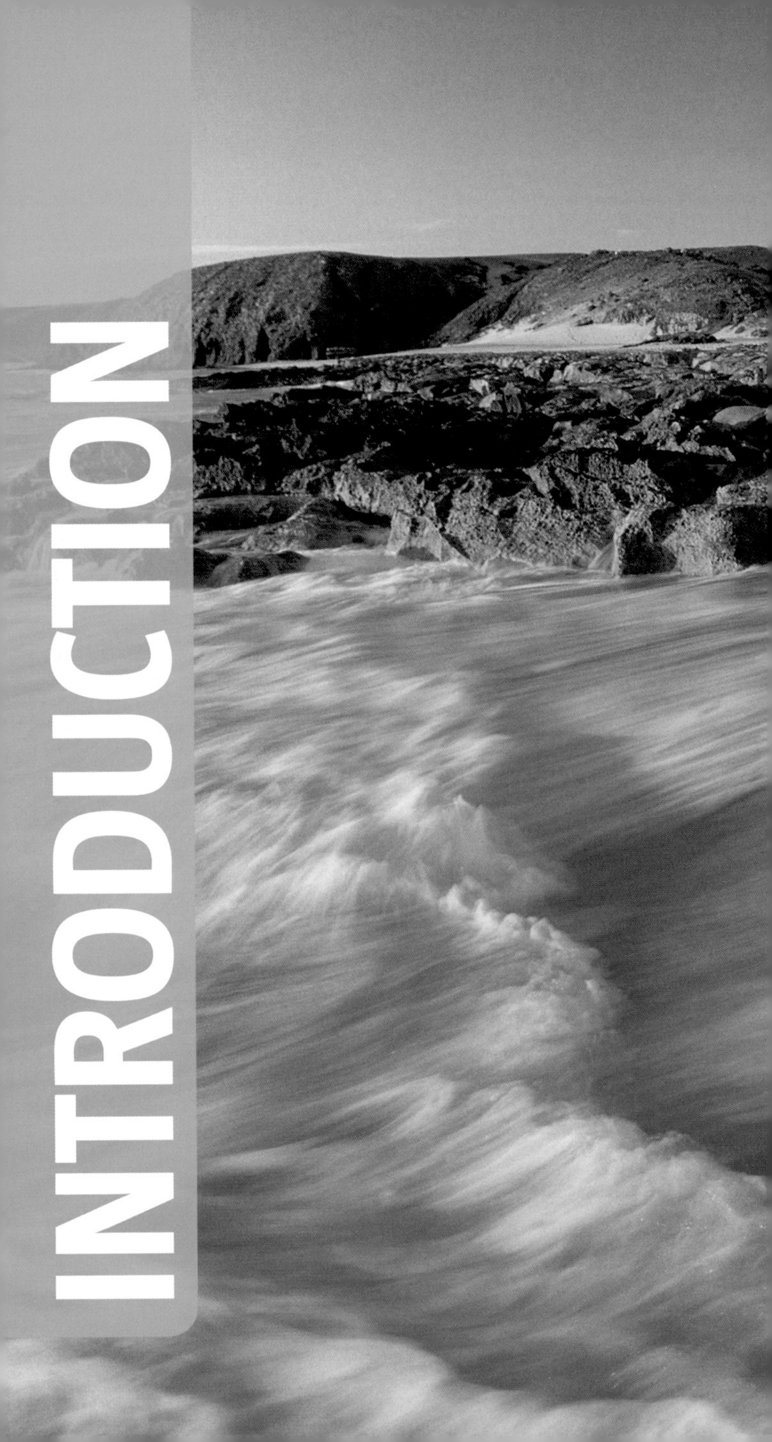

Photo: Puerto del Carmen

DISCOVER LANZAROTE!

Look out the window as your plane descends; it is as if you are arriving on the set for a science-fiction film. Suddenly, emerging from a steel-blue sea, is this picture of bare, beige-grey hills, black fields of lava and craters, a lunar landscape of totally unreal colours and shapes, onto which scudding clouds cast their shadows, while the surging spray of the Atlantic Ocean showers over its shores.

At first sight, Lanzarote looks quite different to the other component parts of the Canary Islands, which, even in antiquity, were fêted as the 'Blessed Islands' because of their benign climate. In some ways the fourth-largest of the seven Islas Canarias resembles a desert. It was in the Tertiary era, over 20 million years ago, when huge volumes of basalt magna broke through the fault lines in the earth's crust to form the two oldest islands in the archipelago, Fuerteventura and Lanzarote. Since then the Canaries have never been totally free of seismic activity. None of the other islands has seen such volcanic turbulence as Lanzarote. Between 1730 and 1736 over 20 percent of the 307 square miles of the island's surface was reconfigured by waves of lava and

The palm trees make all the difference: Haría has an African feel

showers of ash. But it is actually this seemingly bleak, barren and forbidding waste-land that makes Lanzarote unique. Visitors to the volcanic heart of the island with its sparse, bright green vegetation will be confronted with an unparalleled spectacle of the natural world, together with the equally unmistakeable feature of traditional villages with white façades and green windows and doors. The fact that so many settlements radiate in these striking classic colours is due to the work of Lanzarote's most famous son, César Manrique. No other island in the archipelago can boast as many pieces of landscape art by the great painter, sculptor and architect as this land of volcanic fire, which extends for just 37 miles from its north-eastern tip to its south-western corner and only 12.5 miles from east to west.

Before 800 BC
Homer and other poets of antiquity describe the Canary Islands as the 'Islands of the Blessed'

1312
A Genoese navigator, Lancelotto Malocello, lands on Lanzarote and builds a fortress near Teguise. Lanzarote later takes its name from him

1402
The Norman Jean de Béthencourt conquers Lanzarote for the Castilian crown, and subdues the aboriginal population

1433–1479
The Portuguese and the Spanish quarrel over the Canary Islands. The islands are conceded to Spain under the Treaty of Alcáçovas

Despite its small size, the island exhibits a very varied range of landscapes. End-less fields of ash and clinker cover much of the western half of the island. The south is dry and thinly populated, but the golden beaches around El Papagayo are truly idyllic and very popular. The wine-producing areas near La Geria in the centre of the island look odd and out-of-place, while the chalk-white tourist citadels of Puerto del Carmen and Costa Teguise on the east coast are much more in keeping with a holiday island. They surround the island's capi-tal, Arrecife. At the northern end of the island near the small town of Haría, the centre of the island's agricultural region, the scenery is surprisingly colourful and lush. Not to be forgotten, however, are the islands of La Graciosa, Montaña Clara and Alegranza, which appear as splashes of colour dripped onto the north end of Lanzarote's palette.

The mild climate is attributable to the north-east trade winds, which deliver rain to the other islands in the archipelago. Lanzarote's bad luck is that the highest peak, Peñas del Chache in the northern Risco de Famara range, measures only 2200 ft in height, too low to trigger proper rainfall from the clouds. The trade winds help to moderate the heat, as does the Canary Current, a coolish reverse flow in the Gulf Stream system, but life is much harder for the local farmers and vine-growers here than on the other islands. But

> **Lunar landscapes, golden beaches and wines with a difference**

1730–1736
Numerous volcanic eruptions devastate the south of Lan-zarote. Many islanders emi-grate to Latin America

1852
Arrecife becomes the island's capital

1936
General Franco, the military commander of the Canary Islands, stages a coup against the government in Madrid. The Spanish Civil War begins

1960 onwards
Tourism replaces agriculture as the island's main business

1975
Following Franco's death, dem-ocratic government is restored to Spain. Tourism takes off

the inhabitants have always been inventive: *enarenado* is the name for the ingenious method of dry cultivation devised by the Lanzaroteans. Under this system, the volcanic rock absorbs moisture from the air at night, and then releases it into the ground during the day. Little is known about the island's original inhabitants, known as the Majos. They probably came to Lanzarote from North Africa in the 5th century BC or later, and it is believed they are genetically related to the light-skinned Berber peoples who still live there. More recent sources have suggested that the aboriginal Canarians migrated here from the Mediterranean region around Sicily. They lived from fishing and growing cereals, which were ground in primitive mills into *gofio*, a type of flour and the main staple in the diet of the early Canarians. Nowadays, however, it would be impossible for the lanzaroteños to live off farming and fishing alone.

The whole of Lanzarote – a Biosphere Reserve

Most of the 142,000 inhabitants earn their living from the 1.5 million holidaymakers who come to the island every year. Many local people work as receptionists, cooks, porters, cleaners, gardeners or travel guides. The insecure nature of their livelihood stands in stark contrast to the everlasting beauty of the island. The work is mainly seasonal and with unemployment at around 30 percent of the population, all who have a job considers themselves to be very lucky. Most of the people employed in tourism live in the capital, Arrecife, and in the suburbs of Playa Honda and Tías, which have grown dramatically in recent years. The uniform and rather bleak high-rise blocks in the new districts contrast with the pretty villages in the hinterland, where those who have profited from tourism have built luxurious properties.

The wells ran dry a long time ago, so desalination plants now supply the island's drinking water. This is expensive to produce and also to supply. Wind farms reach up to the sky, strips of asphalt snake through the fields of lava. The lanzaroteños have successfully avoided the eyesores that tarnish the vistas in the tourist hotspots on Gran Canaria and Tenerife, thanks largely to the efforts of César Manrique. As a result of his work, in 1993 the island was awarded the coveted Unesco Biosphere Reserve status. Unesco were particularly impressed by the fact that almost 70 percent of the island's surface area – including a large national park – is a protected zone, and that

1986
Spain becomes a member of the European Community, and the Canary Islands a free trade zone

1993
UNESCO awards Biosphere Reserve status to Lanzarote and César Manrique is acclaimed for his achievements

2000 onwards
Despite the imposition of a pause in construction work, more and more large hotels are built, endangering the island's UNESCO Biosphere Reserve status

2010
The financial crisis hits Spain hard. The construction industry collapses and almost 30 percent of all Canarians find themselves out of work

How Lanzarote's most famous son lived: César Manrique's living room

the small offshore archipelago, (Archipiélago Chinijo, which includes La Graciosa, Alegranza and Montaña Clara), has been designated as Spain's first marine reserve. Another positive feature is that a traditional style of architecture in keeping with the landscape predominates, and there are no imported standard structures. However, Unesco is now considering whether to strip Lanzarote of its Biosphere Reserve status. Within only a few years, for example, the small fishing village of Playa Blanca has become a mega holiday resort, and in Las Breñas and Puerto Calero urbanizaciónes or holiday villages for prosperous Europeans have sprung up like mushrooms. In the meantime Spain's highest

> **Pause to let the peace and tranquillity work its magic on you**

court has ruled that almost all the new hotels in Playa Blanca are illegal, as they were built without the appropriate construction licence and in contravention of environmental regulations. But none of the hotel proprietors need fear the imminent demolition of their hotels, which cost millions of euros and were partly funded by EU grants.

Only in hidden corners, in villages well away from the main holiday centres on the south-east coast, does one get the sense that Lanzarote, unlike all the other Canary Islands, is still a place of privation, underemployment and tranquillity. This can often be seen in the faces of the older rural population: farmers with a mule-drawn plough stoically turning over the dusty soil, farmers' wives harvesting fruit from endless rows of prickly pears, old men gathered in the village square idly passing the time of day. The Lanzarote of yesteryear still lives on, and only those who go in search of it with open eyes and receptive ears, pausing as they look and listen, will discover the island's true magic.

WHAT'S HOT

1 Eco-glamping

Stay the night in a yurt There are few camp sites on the island, so if you love to get close to nature, why not spend the night in a Mongolian yurt. If you want to keep up-to-date with current trends, then try camping out in luxuriously equipped tents. It's called 'glamping' (glamour camping). Facilities include wooden furniture, a bed and a seating area. Thanks to the renewable energy supply and an organic garden, you can be confident you are minimising your carbon footprint.

Guests staying at the *Villa Amatista* can expect to spend the night in an original Mongolian yurt suitable for three persons, private terrace included. Food comes from the in-house organic garden, water and energy from environmentally friendly sources *(Camino las Huertitas 11, La VeguetaTinajo, www.villa-amatista.com)*. Another company, *Lanzarote Retreats*, gives guests the choice of different tent sizes and furnishings. All yurts meet environmental sustainability standards, with energy supplied from solar panels and wind turbines *(Calle Diseminado Tabayesco 34 A, Arrieta, www.lanzaroteretreats.com, photo)*.

Mud, water, seaweed

Find harmony Cultivate the body beautiful on Lanzarote by taking advantage of its plentiful supply of black, volcanic earth. The mud is used for beauty applications, the abundant aloe vera and local wines keep the skin supple, and sea salt from Lanzarote's coast cleanses the body. In the *Centro de Terapia Antroposófica* in the Finca Lomos Altos, black volcanic mud is put to good use with massage and peeling therapies *(Calle Salinas 12 E, Puerto del Carmen, www.centro-lanzarote.de)*. At the ● *Princesa Yaiza* seawater works wonders as the essential ingredient in thalassotherapy *(Avda Papagayo 22, Playa Blanca, www.princesayaiza.com)*. In the spa at the *Hesperia Hotel,* Lanzarote's plants, in the form of wine and aloe vera, are applied to the skin to impart a soft and radiant sheen *(Urbanización Cortijo Viejo, Puerto Calero, www.hesperia.com, photo)*.

A different kind of breakfast

Croissants and pastries   Instead of rushing things in the morning by simply downing a strong espresso, many lanzaroteños are now taking it easy and starting the day with a proper breakfast. Upmarket bakeries call themselves *croissantería* or *boutique del pan* (bread boutique) and offer a very wide selection of breakfast specialities. *Pastelito Tahiche* sells traditional pastries from the region and also the sort of pâtisserie that northern Europeans are familiar with (*Avda Nestor de la Torre 22, Tahiche*). *Café Aroma*, on the other hand, will supply sun worshippers with the sustenance required for a day on the beach, such as wraps with a choice of filling or delicious cakes (*Avda Papagayo, Playa Blanca*).

Lanza fashion

A la mode   Young designers have conquered the island with striking designs, and Lanzarote is inspiring the fashion world. More and more designers are opening up studios on the island, using light and airy fabrics for exciting creations in bright and cheerful colours. *Marga Mod* specialises in using delicate materials and fresh, flashy designs (*Calle Sancocho 78, Mozaga, www.margamod.com*). *Maria Cao's* favourite materials are also light. She already works for Armani and Nacho Ruiz, with linen her preferred fabric. Her style is perfect for hot days by the sea and it's also just right for those wanting to take home something distinctive from the island (*Plaza San Francisco 2, Teguise*). Romy Baltensperger, a Lanzarote-based Swiss artist and designer, seeks her inspiration in raw nature and the lightness of being typical of her adopted home. The *RomyB* label can be found at *Moda Indigo* (in the *Galeria La Villa, Placa Clavijo y Fajardo 4, Teguise, www.romyb.info, photo, see p. 80.*)

IN A NUTSHELL

ARCHITECTURE

From cave dwelling to hotel – 1000 years of living on Lanzarote: the early Canarians lived in either caves under the lava or used simple stone tools to dig out a crater and then built an igloo-style roof over the top. Larger tunnel systems, such as the Cueva de los Verdes, were probably used as places of refuge when the island came under attack or natural catastrophes occurred. The island's rulers even built their residences partially underground. One such site has been found near Tahiche.

During the 14th century, the European conquerors initially built fortresses. The oldest one occupied the site of today's Castillo de Guanapay. Later on, Spanish settlers from Andalusia brought the Moorish-inspired mudéjar style, which survives in buildings such as churches and grand villas. Other typical exam-ples of mudéjar architecture are seen in simple façades, bare-brick house corners, tiled roofs, patios and richly ornamented wooden ceilings and balconies. The finest Moorish-style structures are in Teguise and Yaiza, and a number of churches elsewhere on the island.

The peasants of yesteryear had a simple motto: square, practical, strong. The model for this sort of cubed house, still very popular today, comprising thick, white-washed walls, flat roofs and tiny windows, can still be seen in North Africa.

CÉSAR MANRIQUE

Just what couldn't this Arrecife-born polymath do? Painter, sculptor, architect, designer, writer, green activist, César Manrique, born in 1919, was successful in many fields and is, by a long way, Lanzarote's most famous son. After his first exhibitions of representational pictures,

Photo: Cactus fields around Guatiza

How do vines thrive with no rain? Why didn't the dromedaries lose their jobs? What are beetles doing in a cocktail? Lanzarote's secrets unravelled

in 1945 he moved to Madrid, where he discovered abstract art and quickly made a name for himself. In 1965 he left for the USA and stayed there for three years. But when the tourists started arriving on Lanzarote in 1968, he returned, so that he could be in a position to contribute artistically when the modern world arrived in his homeland. Manrique transformed tunnels of lava and caves into breathtakingly beautiful dreamscapes; he built monuments and wind chimes. He campaigned vigorously against a replication of the concrete monsters that had sprung up on the other Canary Islands. What he fought really hard for was the preservation of the island's landscape by promoting its traditional architecture. Facing considerable resistance, he persuaded the authorities to impose strict conditions on new construction work; he designed low-rise holiday villages himself and oversaw the conversion of hotels. Manrique died in a car accident on 26 November 1992 near his home at Tahiche. But the foundation which bears his name, the ☺ *Fundación César Manrique*, ensures that his 'critical voice' continues to be heard. The exhibitions and workshops staged there address a wide range of topics, from art and architecture to globalisation, immigration, environmental protection and nature conservation *(www.fcmanrique.org)*.

COCHINEAL

Many people think it's some sort of bad joke, but it's true. The striking red colouring of Campari comes from beetle blood. If you are not convinced, you can check it out for yourself on Lanzarote. Growing on the many acres of land between Guatiza and Mala is an abundance of prickly (or cactus) pears. The plant's Latin name is opuntia and it is native to Mexico, but it is also the favourite food of the cochineal beetle. And this tiny, grey-white scale insect produces carminic acid, from which the crimson-coloured dye carmine is derived.

The bugs cluster on the cactus leaves, feeding on the plants' sap. They then multiply rapidly. Every two to three months, the new larvae are removed manually from the fiercely prickly opuntia plants using a scraper. When they have been cleaned, they are killed by immersion in hot water, dried, ground and mixed with aluminium or calcium salts. Millions of the insects die to make a kilo of cochineal dye. Initially, the future for cochineal breeding was rosy, but a generation later, after the invention of cheap, synthetic aniline dyes, prospects for the business started to fade. Natural cochineal red is still used in some foods (sweets, liqueurs), cosmetics and medicines. It is one of the few water-soluble colorants that resist degradation with time. Products made using cochineal, e.g. soaps, bath essences and peeling masks, may be purchased in Punta Mujeres *(Aloe Vera House: Mon–Sat 10am–6pm, Sun 10am–5pm | Calle Jameos del Agua s/n | www.aloepluslanzarote.com)*.

DROMEDARIES

It is a truly amazing sight: long caravans picking their way slowly across the ash mountains in the Timanfaya National Park. Lanzarote's dromedaries are among the island's main tourist attractions. These single-humped beasts of burden, also known as the Arabian camel, almost certainly arrived on the island with the first Europeans. They

A rarely-encountered Canarian aborigine – the dragon tree

make perfect working animals, as they can, if necessary, go for weeks without water and will carry heavy loads over long distances without complaint. They were used in the fields to carry goods and to operate gofio mills, and can also be ridden like a horse.

It was thought that the introduction of the combustion engine would end their career. But tourism has given the dromedaries a new lease of life. Now, every day, hundreds of holidaymakers climb into the saddle on the side of the hump and take a rocking ride through the Fire Mountains in the Timanfaya National Park. Dromedaries are bred near the village of Uga. Every afternoon between 4.30pm and 5pm the weary caravan heads home from the National Park – INSIDER TIP▸ photo essential!

FLORA & FAUNA

At first sight Lanzarote might seem totally lifeless. But thousands of wild flowers, many of which only occur on the Canary Islands, can be found growing on the island. These include the spring-flowering, white *tajinaste* (bugloss), the scented, lavender-like *retama* and the sweet and bitter *tabaibas*, squat bushes with fat, sausage-like branches emerging from between the rocks. Hundreds of types of lichen have invaded the lava, breaking down the once-molten rock in a process that takes millennia. The *cardón* is the best-known of the many varieties of euphorbia. Their long, spiny columns tower skyward like candelabra. Canarian date palms, whose overhanging foliage and orange-coloured fruit give the valley around Haría a distinctive African feel, are plants that only thrive on the Canary Islands. But the weirdest of them is all is the *drago*, the dragon tree. Sadly, only a few specimens of this unusual species have survived. A member of the

lily family, it died out practically everywhere over 20 million years ago except on the Macaronesian Islands, i.e. the Canaries, Madeira, the Azores and the Cape Verde Islands. For the early Canarians the dragon tree, with its scaly bark, bizarrely-shaped, thick branches with clusters of sabre-like leaves and a trail

Still very popular – lucha canaria or Canarian wrestling

of cherry-sized fruit, was regarded as sacred because of its precious reddish resin. Known as dragon's blood, this fluid turns dark red when exposed to the air. They used it from early times in the preparation of medicinal potions and ointments. It was later much sought-after as a wood stain and was used to colour Stradivarius violins. As far as imported species are concerned, the survival of the colourful blossom on bougainvilleas, hibiscus bushes, geraniums and poinsettia is attributable largely to intensive irrigation. Only a few forms of animal life survive on Lanzarote. Apart from a few feral cats and dogs, and rabbits and pigeons imported for hunting, the only other creatures are sea birds and birds of prey. The serin with its dark-streaked, greyish

GOAT'S CHEESE

For the early Canarians goats were a very important resource. They supplied milk, cheese, meat, bones and skin. Hardly any effort was required to satisfy these omnivores. In earlier centuries, Lanzarote was a harsh environment and life was a hard slog. However, goats can pose a number of problems. Many thousands of these animals roam more or less unmanaged throughout the countryside and consume practically anything edible, thereby destroying the island's already sparse vegetation. Nevertheless the lively herds with their jangling bells are an ever-present feature of the landscape. Do make a point of sampling the *queso de cabra* (goat's cheese), one of Lanzarote's few culinary specialities. It is produced in small cheese dairies, often from unpasteurised milk. Despite requiring only three basic ingredients, milk, rennet and salt, somehow the finished product reveals a wide variety of subtly differing flavours. There are cheese dairies near Teguise, in Femés and in Uga. The last-mentioned farm sells its products in the *Bodega Stratvs (see p. 68)* and has regularly picked up prizes at international competitions, notably a World Cheese Award. At regional level, its *queso rojillo* was nominated out of 140 different varieties as the best cheese on the Canary Islands because of its flavour and presentation. It is a semi-cured, creamy cheese made from pasteurised goat's milk. A coating of paprika on the rind gives the cheese a distinctive spicy flavouring. *Rojillo* means 'reddish', the same name as Lanzarote's football team.

LUCHA CANARIA

Lucha canaria or *Canarian wrestling* has been a popular pursuit on the island since the days of the early Canarians. This is a sport that is only practised on the islands

One of César Manrique's legacies: the Guatiza cactus garden

green plumage and yellow rump is an ancestor of the colourful canary. A type of shrew, named the Canary shrew and found only here, was discovered a few decades ago. Also unique are the white crabs which live in the cave pools at the Jameos del Agua. Barely two centimetres long, the albino Munidopsis polymorpha, which resembles a miniature lobster complete with claws, has existed in complete darkness for so long that it has no eyes. It can be seen as it forages for food in the cave's clear waters.

of the Canarian archipelago, and thrilling contests are still held today. A team consists of twelve wrestlers, but they only fight in pairs within a ring 40 feet in diameter and covered with sawdust or sand. Battle commences from a starting position, i.e. leaning forward facing the opponent with his or her trouser leg in the left hand. Each contest lasts a maximum of three minutes. The *luchadores*, as the wrestlers are known, grasp their opponent using a variety of holds, the object being to grapple the opponent down, so that any part of the body, except the feet, touches the sand. But what is required is not just strength. Technique and speed are also decisive. There are no weight categories as in boxing. It is possible for a 55 kg lightweight to be facing a colossus weighing twice as much. In this case, the skill lies in using subtle ploys to get the better of a cumbersome opponent. For some time now, women have also been involved in the sport. If an opponent is floored twice in a maximum of three fights, then the victor wins a point and the defeated wrestler has to drop out. The team that still has wrestlers on the bench at the end wins the competition.

Should you wish to be a spectator at a INSIDER TIP Canarian wrestling match, there are arenas *(terrero de lucha)* in Tinajo, Uga, Yaiza, Playa Blanca and Tahiche. The competitions are usually held at the weekend, but an up-to-date listing of events is available from the tourist information office or you can visit *www.lucha canarialanzarote.com* (only in Spanish).

MALVASIA

Possibly as early as the 15th century, vines from Crete reached the Canary Islands. The first documented evidence of vines growing on Lanzarote dates from 1600. The earthy, full-bodied fruitiness of the bright, sun-drenched Canary grape rapidly won over the palates of mainland Europeans. The wines went down particularly well in England — at least until the first barrels of port and sherry came ashore. Only after the volcanic eruptions of the 18th century, when enarenado, the method of dry cultivation, was introduced, did interest revive. Now about 40 percent of Lanzarotean wines come from the Malvasia grape. The current varieties are a dry white table wine with fruity notes and *moscatel*, a dessert wine. In both cases, look out for *denominación de origen* on the label. This serves as proof of its origin.

WATER

Water is a most precious commodity on Lanzarote. In the past, the islanders took their drinking water from wells, fed from the Famara Mountains along a system of tunnels *(galerías)* to the settlements where it was needed, or else they collected rainwater in tanks, known as *aljibes*. The largest of these underground reservoirs, the *gran mareta*, was in Teguise.

But because of growing demand and the depletion of groundwater supplies, now some 90 percent of drinking water is taken from the sea. To desalinate 1000 litres of water, some 8 litres of heating oil is required, a huge drain on resources. But at least the new desalination plants use the reverse osmosis process, i.e. the salt is removed from the seawater mechanically. An added issue is that a holiday visitor uses on average twice as much drinking water as a native. But no longer is purified drinking water used to water the plantings in the many holiday complexes and on public open spaces. Treatment plants cleanse all waste water, so that it can be recycled. Ingenious piping systems ensure efficient distribution. So one important plea should be heeded by all visitors: use water sparingly.

FOOD & DRINK

It is often said that Canarian cuisine lacks sophistication. The islanders have honed their inventive skills over the years, in order to conjure up a delicious meal from very little.

The Lanzaroteans have had to overcome many hardships in their long history. No one could deny that. Dry soil and a scorching sun, and yet the people have always managed to put food on the plate. Canarian cuisine grew out of poverty. Lanzarote's aboriginal inhabitants survived mainly on *gofio*, a flour produced from roasted grains of barley or maize. First the grains were crushed and then ground into flour in windmills. The beige-coloured or light-brown powder had a more or less unlimited shelf-life; it was versatile, rich in protein and also filling.

The Majos always kept a sack of *gofio* in the kitchen and with it they created a wide range of nourishing dishes: it was baked into bread, stirred into soup and drinks, added to fish, meat or potatoes or mixed with honey and almonds as a dessert. Daily life without *gofio* was unimaginable. It is still produced and served up at the table, but nowadays the powder is made only from wheat or maize. In the era of pasta and burgers, *gofio* is no longer such an important staple.

On the other hand, soups and stews have retained their status as everyday fare. A *potaje*, that famous vegetable soup into which the cook stirred anything that lived or grew, is still to be found on the menu in every restaurant that serves *cocina casera* or what we might call home cooking.

Photo: *Papas arrugadas* with *mojo rojo*, red sauce

Barren land, a scorching sun – but you can still look forward to a varied menu of countless culinary creations

Puchero and *rancho canario* are heartier. Into these thicker stews goes the meat from chickens, cattle or pigs. Not to be forgotten is the ropa vieja, literally old laundry. The name quaintly, but clearly, refers to the origins of this country delicacy, i.e. the week's leftovers. Nothing was ever wasted.

Influences from other parts of the world – the Canary Islands archipelago was once at the crossroads of international trade – are still to be found in the *cocina canaria*. Yams from Africa, sweet potatoes from South America and saffron from La Mancha appear in everyday dishes.

Meat and fish used to be served only on special occasions. Every goat was precious, as it supplied milk. The Canarian sun has always limited food storage times, and the Spanish settlers had to cope with this problem too. So any booty that arrived in the household was pickled in sea salt and turned into a spicy concoction known as adobos, marinades, in which fish and meat did not spoil. These typically Canarian sauces made from oil,

LOCAL SPECIALITIES

▶ **arroz a la cubana** – boiled white rice with fried banana, fried egg and tomato sauce; a simple meal with a Caribbean influence, popular also in the Philippines and Peru.

▶ **bienmesabe** – sticky, golden brown dessert made from honey, slivers of almond, egg yolk and lemon. Translates as 'tastes good to me' and that is most people's reaction

▶ **caldo de pescado** – a watery fish soup with potatoes and herbs

▶ **carajacas** – liver of veal, pork or chicken, chopped and marinated in a hot *adobo* (marinade or seasoning)

▶ **cherne al cilantro** – pan-fried Canarian gilthead bream in a spicy coriander sauce

▶ **gambas al ajillo** – prawns deep-fried in olive oil with garlic, chillies and parsley

▶ **gofio escaldado** – *gofio* (roasted cereals) with a *caldo de pescado* stock thickened into a velvety, maize-yellow porridge, served with herbs and bell peppers

▶ **leche asada** – milk pudding, mixed with eggs, lemon peel, cinnamon and sugar

▶ **mojo rojo** – red *mojo*: smooth to runny hot dip made with red peppers (photo right), oil, garlic, vinegar and salt, and served with meat dishes and *papas arrugadas*

▶ **mojo verde** – green *mojo*: same method as *mojo rojo,* but with green peppers and lots of coriander leaves, to accompany fish dishes and *papas arrugadas*

▶ **papas arrugadas** – baby Canarian potatoes boiled in salted water, always eaten with their wrinkled skins *(arrugado*; photo left); delicious with mojos or grilled fish

▶ **pella** – loaf made from gofio, water and salt. Cut into slices and eaten with *sancocho canario*

▶ **rancho canario** – hearty stew made from chick peas, potatoes, pork, pasta, onions, saffron, garlic, pepper sausage; sometimes served as a starter

▶ **sancocho canario** – boiled, salted fish, usually eaten with vegetables and mojo; the traditional dish for Good Friday

vinegar, bay leaves, herbs and garlic are regarded as distinctive features in the island's cuisine.

Small but nippy fishing boats cast their nets into the waters off Lanzarote's coast and haul out *cherne, bocinegro* and *vieja*. All are species peculiar to the Canary Islands and many of them quickly make it into the island's kitchens. Tuna and sardines are always worth recommending. Usually they are served simply *a la plancha*, after sizzling in hot oil on a metal plate. The same is true of seafood. *Choco* (squid) and *pulpo* (octopus) are snacks eaten only with fresh white bread. And then there are *papas arrugadas* and *mojo*, Canarian specialities much loved by tourists.

Tapas are just as popular on Lanzarote as they are on the Spanish mainland. These 'lite bites' have now found their way into the simple bars and cafeterias, where lanzaroteños take breakfast and lunch. In the morning, it is usually enough just to order a *café solo* or a *cortado*, a small black aromatic coffee served with or without milk, plus a *bocadillo* (a large roll with a topping). At lunch time, i.e. from 1pm, it is the custom to sit at the bar by the tapas display cabinet and snack on a little bowl of *albóndigas* (meatballs in sauce), *boquerones* (anchovies), eaten deep-fried or *en vinagre,* or any other delicacies on offer.

In the evenings lanzaroteños devote time to their families. The evening meal eaten together with family does not usually begin until about 10pm. Suppers usually consist of light fare, which includes tapas, salad and white bread, occasionally fish or potaje.

Many families treat themselves at the weekend. After a day on the beach comes a meal in a restaurant, followed by the luxury of a dessert, perhaps even a bottle of wine. Lanzarote is – just after Tenerife – the largest wine producer in the Canarian archipelago. In recent years, many family-owned cellars have been modernised and new bodegas have opened. At the same time, the quality of the product has improved dramatically and the wines frequently win international prizes. Along the La Geria wine route, many bodegas open for wine tastings and visitors are also invited to

The taste of Lanzarote:
white wine from La Geria

take tours through the cellars (see p. 68). By the way, lanzaroteños also love their beer. Canarian brands such as *Dorada* and *Tropical* fully meet international expectations. A large bottle of mineral water is an essential accompaniment to every meal.

For the locals cloth serviettes, bread and butter and performances of traditional folk music are not part of a restaurant meal. These frills are purely for tourists. It's much better to see out the evening in traditional style: with a bottle of La Geria wine and a carajillo, a strong and tasty espresso with a shot of brandy.

SHOPPING

The local markets are always a festival of colour, notably the Sunday market in Teguise. This little town is transformed into a bazaar of curiosities and kitsch, with crafts and culinary delights among the main draws. Usually the vendor is also the producer. It could be an elderly señor selling hand-crafted cane baskets or an ageing hippie behind a table overflowing with lava jewellery. Arts and crafts have a long tradition on Lanzarote, but the skills only survive thanks to the tourist trade. The market in Teguise proved to be so successful that many more *mercadillos* or mini-markets have since appeared on the scene: in Costa Teguise on a Friday evening, in Arrecife, Haría and Playa Blanca on Saturday morning.

The local people are more likely to do their shopping in Playa Honda, a suburb of Arrecife. Here warehouse and outlet stores line the LZ-2 highway; not exactly sumptuous palaces of consumerism, but still very functional sales halls. You will find pretty well everything you are familiar with at home, but here it will probably be considerably cheaper.

ART

Lanzarote is very lucky to have as one of its heroes César Manrique, the best-known painter, sculptor and architect in the Canary Islands. He was a genius, who even twenty years after his death still inspires, even dominates, the art world. An international community of artists has since established itself on the holiday island. Their studios are to be found in a number of places including Arrecife, Yaiza and Teguise. For further information, please ask at the tourist information offices. Teseguite is home to the splendid workshop and gallery **INSIDER TIP** *Arte y Cerámica (Mon–Fri 11am–5pm| Av. Acorán 43–45 | tel. 928 84 56 50 | www.aguttenberger.com)*.

EMBROIDERY

First and foremost comes eyelet and hem-stitch embroidery, known as calados. If you pay a visit to the *Taller Municipal de Artesanía (Sat 10am–2.30pm)* in Haría, you can watch how the delicate blankets, bedspreads, curtains and other textile are created. One of Lanzarote's last basket-weavers also works there. The palm trees in the immediate vicinity supply the raw material for baskets and also straw hats.

FINE FOODS

Lanzarote's popular wine with its distinc-

Lanzarote's crafts have adapted to suit visitors' tastes. But it's still fun rummaging around in the markets.

tive strong and fruity flavour is available in all supermarkets, but if you want a better selection, you are advised to purchase from the bodega. Please note that the local wines are not suitable for storing. One unusual and original product is sea salt from the Salinas de Janubio. It is sold in small, decorative packs.

Goat's cheese is just as much a delicacy as the hot and spicy mojo sauces. The latter are sold in preserving jars. The sweet dessert known as bienmesabe is sold in similar glass packaging. The above souvenirs may be bought in supermarkets, as can ron miel. This honey rum is another Canarian speciality, but most of it comes from the neighbouring island of Gran Canaria.

POTTERY

Pottery is produced in the traditional way without a potter's wheel. The clay must first be worked into manageable lengths. The potter lays the lengths on top of each other, then they are rolled out and any unevenness smoothed with a sharp stone.

The natural umbra or russet colour in bowls and jugs has not been painted on. Tourists want colourful souvenirs, so many plates and bowls are now sold in fresh and bright colours. Clay fertility figurines in early Canarian style make very popular souvenirs, with many holidaymakers bemused and amused by their erotic details.

TIMPLES

Teguise is the centre of timple production. These five-stringed instruments that closely resemble guitars are also decorative masterpieces. Made by hand, they are usually adorned with elaborate inlay work. Timples still play an important part in the island's festivals. No celebration, no performance of folk music, no singing or dance event can take place without accompaniment by these Canarian-style ukeleles. The timples seen on sale in markets and bazaars, on the other hand, are industrially produced. Lanzarotean *artesanía* is not inferior merchandise. The prices charged reflect the time, effort and skills of the makers.

THE PERFECT ROUTE

LAVA & AGRICULTURE

Flows of black lava, cones and craters: In the ① *Parque Nacional de Timanfaya* → p. 72 a tour bus will take you on a sightseeing tour of the Fire Mountain; at the ② *Centro de Visitantes* → p. 75 in Mancha Blanca, you get an introduction to the mysteries of the volcano. On the other hand, the ③ *Museo Agrícola El Patio* → p. 71, a beautifully furnished farmhouse dating from 1845 and surrounded by a sub-tropical garden, reveals the secrets of rural life from the time of the early settlers. The ④ *Monumento al Campesino* → S. 69 is a reminder of the current problems facing farmers. Traditional handicraft products are on sale nearby.

MONASTERIES, CHURCHES AND A CHAPEL

With its white houses, monasteries and churches, the old capital, ⑤ *Teguise* → p. 52 is the town with the longest history on the island. Take a stroll through this little treasure trove of colonial architecture, before you feast your eyes on the fine view from the ⑥ *Ermita de las Nieves* → p. 57. This tiny chapel stands guard on the island's highest peak, offering an impressive view of Lanzarote's west coast.

GET OUT INTO THE COUNTRYSIDE

Now we head downhill, deep into the Valley of a Thousand Palms, a part of the island that becomes an oasis after rainfall. At its heart lies the pretty village of ⑦ *Haría* → p. 57, which springs into life during the Sunday market. But the road quickly starts to climb again. Where Lanzarote drops into the sea as if chopped by an axe, you can look forward to some breathtaking views through the panoramic window of the ⑧ *Mirador del Río* → p. 58 over the straits between Lanzarote and the island of La Graciosa. Now fortify yourself in one of the restaurants at the fishing village of ⑨ *Órzola* → p. 48, where the seafood on offer blends perfectly with the dry wines of Monte Corona.

GOING UNDERGROUND

Now it gets exciting! Enter the ⑩ *Jameos del Agua* → p. 47 through a vast hole in the blanket of volcanic lava. This remarkable geological feature comprises a system of tunnels that César Manrique transformed into an enchanting natural spectacle. Also underground here is the ⑪ *Cueva de los Verdes* → p.46. The tour though this multi-coloured labyrinth of caves to the accompaniment of celestial music takes about 45 minutes – be prepared for at least one surprise!

Discover the many different faces of Lanzarote from north to south and from east to west, plus a few short detours to sights of breathtaking beauty

THE MASTER'S TREASURES

A Manrique wind chime, an aloe vera museum and a short walk make **12** *Arrieta* → p. 45 a very welcome stopping point. An oversized steel cactus in Guatiza points the way to César Manrique's final piece. The **13** *Jardín de Cactus* → p. 46 is a botanical garden containing a huge collection of spiny plants. The maestro's former residence is now the **14** *Fundación César Manrique* → p. 48, an astonishing house that has been created within a series of volcanic bubbles. It's a sight you won't forget easily.

NATURAL PHENOMENA & BEAUTY SPOTS

Also unforgettable is the journey through the valley of **15** *La Geria* → p. 68 with its thousands of craters, in which the grapes ripen. By all means sample and buy the wines in the bodegas. **16** *Yaiza* → p. 86, the blueprint for Lanzarotean architecture, shines out in white and green from the dark landscape, while the deep green of the lagoon at **17** *El Golfo* → p. 83 has an almost otherworldly aura. Two other natural attractions round off the tour: In **18** *Los Hervideros* → p. 84 Atlantic waves crash dramatically through blowholes, and the view over the geometric salt flats at **19** *Salinas de Janubio* → p. 85 is another bizarre sight.

90 miles. Journey time: 3 hours. Detailed map of the route on the back cover, in the road atlas and the pull-out map

ARRECIFE

CITY **WHERE TO START?**

WHERE TO START?
Seaside promenade: The best place to start a stroll through Lanzarote's capital is the seaside promenade. Park your car near the promenade (e.g. in the underground car-park of the Gran Hotel Arrecife); the town is quite small, but the congestion can be frustrating. If you are arriving in Arrecife by bus, then get out at the promenade. Start to walk along the beach as far as the information office *(Mon–Fri 10am–2pm)*, which is close to the Castillo. Head inland along the León y Castillo pedestrianised street, which is close to the Charco harbour area.

MAP INSIDE THE BACK COVER
Late morning in Calle León y Castillo is the time and place to witness the hustle and bustle of Lanzarotean life. Business people, mothers with children on their right hand and shopping bag in their left, señoritas in their lightweight outfits, Canarian señores with their traditional wide-brimmed hats.

Arrecife *(125 C–D5) (Ø F 10)*, a town of 57,000 residents, is no place for lovers of classical colonial architecture. But if you are curious to know more about life on one of the Canary Islands' capitals, then this is the place to come.

As you drive in from the airport via the southern motorway, the changing character of the city becomes evident. First open and spacious, then narrow and

Photo: The Iglesia de San Ginés in Arrecife

The island's capital has had a facelift. Its little lanes and alleyways are an open-air stage on which the everyday life of the local people is enacted.

confined, a paradox that is typical of Canarian town planning. The wide highway whisks you almost as far as the city centre; turn right and suddenly you are in a narrow alley. A little further on to the left and before you know it you will find yourself in the congested traffic chaos of the promenade beside the Playa del Reducto. Overlooking the Avenida Mancomunidad is the five-star Gran Hotel, a high-rise block that was left in ruins for twenty years after a fire. Considerable investment was required to restore it to its present grandeur.

The park, once the favourite haunt of the local drug-taking community, has undergone a full-scale refurbishment and is now a large open space with a boardwalk leading down to the water. Smart yachts are tied to the gold-gleaming bollards that line the shore. The Islote de Fermina, a rocky outcrop stretching far into the sea, has also been upgraded. A number of attractive pools, the designs for which were inspired by César Manrique, have been created at its broad tip: white as snow, with sweeping contours and a view out to sea.

Follow the coast road to the north, and after passing the Club Náutico you come to the Parque Municipal, an elongated plaza with trees, gardens and coloured paving, now a lively and attractive promenade. The Kiosco de la Música in this park, also known as the Parque José Ramírez Cerdá, is the town's tourist information office. the small workshops. But don't worry. Nothing is very far away. With its benches and shady laurel trees, the small plaza in front of the church is the perfect place to sit down and take a break.

Arrecife's jewel in the crown lies in the quarter behind the church and the market, barely visible from the tower of the

El Brujo: works of art in the Castillo de San Gabriel inspired by early Canarian legends

Calle León y Castillo starts on the other side of the road. This pedestrianised zone with its narrow alleyways takes you deep into the vibrant heart of urban Arrecife.

The Castillo's ramparts end with the Puente de Bolas, literally the 'cannonball bridge'. Actually a drawbridge, it has become a symbol for the town of Arrecife. From here stroll on along the Avenida Coll passing a finely restored townhouse with traditional Canarian lattice windows, the Casa de los Arroyo. Overlooking it at the rear between the houses is the tower of the Church of San Ginés. The way to it might look simple. You can easily get lost in the labyrinth of alleyways between the white façades, so a good sense of direction is required, or you may quickly find yourself in a rear courtyard or in one of Castillo: the Charco de San Ginés, the small natural harbour. At the eastern end is the fishing port, where soon after sunrise large and colourful fishing boats arrive back in port with last night's catch. Later on in the day, the fishermen will be out mending their nets, applying a fresh coat of paint to their boats or preparing bait for their next outing.

A few hundred metres out of town, perched on a rocky cliff top, stands the small Castillo de San José, which now marks Arrecife's north-eastern boundary.

SIGHTSEEING

CASTILLO DE SAN GABRIEL

It's obvious that the construction of this small but solid castle dates back many years. The nobleman Don Agustín de Herrera y Royas started work in the second half of the 16th century, soon after the notorious Algerian pirate, Dogali, wreaked havoc in the town, pillaging and murdering here many times. The present building with bell tower and sentry date from 1590. The fortification, where changing exhibitions are staged, can be reached on foot by two long embankments. *Tue–Sat 9am–2pm | admission free*

CASTILLO DE SAN JOSÉ ★ ● ☀

Another castle occupies a more elevated location above the fishing harbour. It was built between 1774 and 1779, when the era of piracy in this part of the world was almost over. However, a long drought at the time was making living conditions very tough, so the project was more about job creation. Now the restored vaults with stout, metres-thick walls accommodate the *Museo Internacional de Arte Contemporáneo*, the Museum of Contemporary Art (MIAC). The names of the artists with works displayed here reads like a Who's Who of classical Spanish modern art: Joan Miró, Antonio Tápies and Pablo Picasso, to name but a few. One room is dedicated to Pancho Lasso (1904–73), Lanzarote's most celebrated sculptor of the 20th century. Temporary exhibitions bring visitors up-to-date with the latest international trends. A fine restaurant with a panoramic view and bearing the same name as the castle occupies the lower floor. Make sure you pay a visit to the viewing platform. *Follow the coast road in the direction of Costa Teguise | museum daily 11am–9pm | admission 2.50 euros*

EL CHARCO DE SAN GINÉS ★ ☀

The harbour in the centre of Arrecife is a fine example of how to redevelop a run-down urban area. Bobbing up and down on the shallow water are brightly coloured fishing boats, which blend in with the striking blue and white houses beside the promenade to form a pretty picture. Years ago the Charco fulfilled in every respect the full meaning of the Spanish word: charco means puddle, and this harbour was indeed a dirty, dilapidated brackish pool, where rubbish and abandoned boats accumulated. The town authorities have successfully managed to smarten up this small natural harbour. The promenade around the basin has been widened and the houses overlooking it have had a comprehensive facelift. During the day the Charco is a lovely place for a stroll, while in the evening

★ **Castillo de San José**
As well as the strangely squat castle, there is also the admirable Museum of Contemporary Art and a stylish restaurant
→ p. 35

★ **El Charco de San Ginés**
This attractively renovated natural harbour has been transformed into a lively bar and restaurant quarter, surrounded by a pedestrian zone. → p. 35

★ **Iglesia de San Ginés**
This plain basilica is situated beside an evocative, laurel-shaded plaza on the fringes of the Charco de San Ginés → p. 36

★ **Altamar**
An impressive place to eat on the 17th floor of the Arrecife Gran Hotel. With its stunning views along the coast, this is just the place for your farewell meal
→ p. 36

MARCO POLO HIGHLIGHTS

the bars open their doors and on a warm day the waiters arrange tables and chairs outside to create an inviting atmosphere.

IGLESIA DE SAN GINÉS ⭐
The town's main church dominates the quiet lanes and alleys in the quarter between El Charco de San Ginés and Calle León y Castillo. The white basilica blends in well with the small, tree-lined Plaza de las Palmas. In the cool interior, the beautiful wooden ceiling in mudéjar style, the black columns of lava stone and the stone, circular arches supporting the roof beams, create a warm atmosphere. *No fixed opening times*

PARQUE MUNICIPAL
The extended promenade with stands of palm trees and beds of exotic plants is an oasis of tranquillity which affords a fine view out to sea. There is a well-equipped playground and a skating park. Buses from Playa Blanca, Puerto del Carmen and Costa Teguise stop on the northern side of the Parque Municipal. This INSIDER TIP small bus terminal *(intercambiador de guaguas)* is worth noting, as the footpath to the town centre, which starts here, is a much shorter route than the one from the central bus station.

PESCADERÍA MUNICIPAL
During the morning the small municipal fish market sells freshly caught fish. *Mon–Sat 8am–1pm | Corner of Calle Liebre/Avda Vargas*

FOOD & DRINK

ALTAMAR ⭐ ☆
A dining room with a breathtaking view along the coast and out to sea from the 17th floor of the Arrecife Gran Hotel. The cuisine is sophisticated and international. Of a high standard, but with matching prices. *Daily | Parque Islas Canarias s/n | tel. 928 80 00 00 | www.arrecifehoteles. com | Expensive*

BAR SAN FRANCISCO
Where every lanzeroteño stops off, when in town on business or shopping in the central area. The brightly tiled restaurant bar is always busy, from the first *café cortado* in the morning until the last glass of wine is poured in the evening. Wide selection of tapas. *Closed Sun | Calle León y Castillo 10am–noon | tel. 928 81 33 83 | Budget*

BODEGÓN LOS CONEJEROS
Reached via a narrow alleyway, this rather rustic-style restaurant serves authentic Lanzarote cuisine to a discerning clientele. *Daily 8pm–2am | Avda Dr. Rafael González 9*

CAFÉ LA UNIÓN ●
Of all the cafés on Plaza de la Constitución, this is by far the most welcoming. With its marble bistro tables and chairs à la Thonet, crystal chandeliers and paintings, it has all the charm of a classic coffee house. Opposite stands the small and rather inconspicuous INSIDER TIP *Sala José Saramago*, a branch of the Fundación César Manrique. Art exhibitions are staged here at irregular intervals. It is named after the winner of the 1998 Nobel Prize for Literature, José Saramago, who died in 2010. He spent the last few years of his life on Lanzarote. *Closed Sun | Plaza de la Constitución 16 | Budget*

CASTILLO DE SAN JOSÉ ☆
Dine out in a castle! The entrance of black lava steps and subtly illuminated walls looks inviting. Panoramic windows reveal a great view over the harbour area, while liveried waiters suggest luxury and sophistication. If you don't want to eat,

but just want to savour the atmosphere at the bar, it's perfectly in order to go in and request a *café con leche. Daily | tel. 928 81 23 21 | Expensive*

to grand celebration cakes. *Closed Sat evening and Sun | Avda Dr. Rafael González 5 | Budget*

Tasty delicacies: the art of the pâtissier on display in the Pastelería Lolita

COFRADÍA DE PESCADORES SAN GINÉS
Restaurant and bar for the fishing co-operative. Freshly prepared fish, lively atmosphere. *Daily | Avda Naos 20 | tel. 608 22 33 34 | Moderate*

INSIDER TIP LILIUM ☼
Gastro bar serving great cuisine. Señor Orlando serves creative island dishes and quality wines by the glass. On weekdays there is an inexpensive menu, but by prior arrangement diners may try out the novel idea of 'blind dining', i.e. eating blindfold, so total concentration on the taste buds is required. *Sun closed | Calle José Antonio 103 | tel. 928 52 49 78 | www.restaurantelilium.com | Moderate*

PASTELERÍA LOLITA
The very best that Arrecife's pâtissiers can offer in cakes and pastries: from sweet gofio variations with honey and peanuts

INSIDER TIP STAR'S CITY ☼
The pub/café on the 17th floor of the Arrecife Gran Hotel can boast not just a fine view over the island's capital but also a superb selection of drinks. *Daily | Parque Islas Canarias s/n | www.arrecifehoteles.com | Budget*

SHOPPING

INSIDER TIP FRIDAY AND SATURDAY MARKET
Every Friday there is a craft market around the information office in front of the Castillo de San Gabriel. And it continues on Saturday morning, when market stalls in the narrow lanes around the church sell a miscellany of food and drink. *Fri/Sat 9am–noon | Calle León y Castillo*

EL MERCADILLO
A small retail centre with shops around a covered patio. Delicious fresh pastries

served in a friendly cafeteria. *Calle León y Castillo 16*

PERFUMERÍA DALIA
A large modern shop with a wide selection of international perfumes and cosmetics. *Calle León y Castillo 24*

SAPHIR JOYEROS
The best jeweller on the island also sells exclusive watches. *In the Arrecife Gran Hotel*

ENTERTAINMENT

The discos on Calle José Antonio don't fill up until after midnight and then only at the weekend. On the harbour promenade and the Playa del Reducto the *cervecerías* (bars selling mainly beer) with open terraces are very popular.

INSIDER TIP BIOSFERA
Covering this large disco, situated south of the Playa del Reducto near the island's government buildings, is a large dome, facing out to sea. Revellers spill out on to the promenade when it gets crowded. Central bar, all the latest pop music, pool tables, darts and other forms of entertainment. Only really gets going after 2am. *Fri–Sun from 10pm | Avda Fred Olsen s/n | www.labiosfera.com*

INSIDER TIP CINE BUÑUEL
The El Almacén cultural centre is attached to this independent cinema. Themed film evenings held usually Wednesday and Thursday. *Calle José Betancort 33 | www.cabildodelanzarote.com*

MULTICINES ATLÁNTIDA
Four modern cinema halls, often showing international films – sometimes dubbed in Spanish, sometimes in the original with Spanish subtitles. *C.C. Atlántida | Calle León y Castillo s/n*

OCOCO / DIVINO DOBLÓN
'In' venue on the Calle José Antonio disco strip. The atmosphere in Ococo warms up to progressive house music. It then changes to contrasting *Divino*, with the DJs keeping the animated throng fired up until late into the night. *Thu–Sat from midnight | Calle José Antonio 62/57 | www.ococo.es*

WHERE TO STAY

ARRECIFE GRAN HOTEL ☼
160 ultra-modern rooms and suites in a first-class hotel in the town centre. With its spectacular view from the higher floors, own pool and spa, it makes INSIDER TIP a stay in the island's capital a realistic alternative to one of the holiday centres. *Parque Islas Canarias s/n | tel. 928 80 00 00 | www.arrecifehoteles. com | Moderate–Expensive*

LANCELOT ☼
The 110 rooms in this hotel are modern, functional and all of them have telephone, safe and TV. Some have a sea view and there's a swimming pool on the roof. *Avda Mancomunidad 9 | tel. 928 80 50 99 | www.hotellancelot.com | Moderate*

A romantic spot in central Arrecife: sunset by the Charco de San Ginés

RESIDENCIA CARDONA

More basic, adequately furnished town hotel at reasonable prices in a central location. The 60 rooms are clean, the bathrooms functional. Communal kitchenette for making tea and coffee. *Calle 18 de Julio 11 | tel. 928 81 10 08 | www. hrcardona.com | Budget*

INSIDER TIP ▶ VILLA VIK

This villa used to belong to an art-lover and is located just outside the town, but is still within easy walking distance of the central area via the seaside promenade. This five-star boutique hotel is designed in a modern, practical style with classical touches, further enhanced by natural stone and stylish furniture. Suites with jacuzzi, plus large garden pool. Top chef Paul Rodbourne is renowned for his creativity. *14 rooms | Calle Hermanos Díaz Rijo 3 | Urbanización La Bufona | Playa del Cable | tel. 928 815256 | www.villavik. com | Expensive*

INFORMATION

Tourist office in the *Parque José Ramírez Cerdá | tel. 928 813174 | www.turismo arrecife.com*

WHERE TO GO

PLAYA HONDA (124 C5) *(Ɱ F 10)*

A fine mile-long beach of golden sand just west of Arrecife town centre, behind it the suburb of the same name in close proximity to Lanzarote's airport. Good shops for fashion, shoes, sport and photographic supplies are to be found in the *Centro Comercial Deiland*. The *Hiper Dino* supermarket sells fresh kitchen herbs.

LOW BUDGET

▶ The *Cafeteria Los Angeles (daily | Calle Ruperto Negrín 6 | tel. 928 81 23 17)* at the heart of the town serves typical Canarian fare, good value tapas and platos combinados.

▶ Stay at the *Pensión San Ginés (37 rooms | Calle El Molino 9 | tel. 928 81 23 51)* near the Charco de San Ginés. A basic double room costs between 20 and 25 euros.

COSTA TEGUISE
AND THE NORTH

Exploring the north from the holiday town of Costa Teguise, you will encounter the many sides of Lanzarote. En route to the old capital of Teguise, you will see how the landscape changes in colour to the brownish beige of the ash fields and the sharp-edged lava rock.

The many chambers and caves were once inhabited by early islanders; today they are often used as stables. Among the dusty hills, villages of white-washed houses survive. Beyond Teguise the terrain changes, becoming more colourful. Here around Los Valles with its pretty terraced fields, the agricultural region begins. It benefits from its position at the foot of the Famara mountain range, which extends to the northern tip of Lanzarote. Here the trade wind clouds

trigger vital rainfall. The panoramic road winds up through fields of vegetables to a height of 2200 ft, passing the 😊 *Parque Eólico de Lanzarote.* The dozens of wind turbines here produce a third of the power needed for desalination plants in Arrecife. In the west sheer cliffs drop 1960 ft to the sea, while in the east the 12-million-year-old mountains run gently down to the coast.

During volcanic eruptions in the 18th century, the inhabitants of the Timanfaya region fled over the windswept *Risco de Famara* to Haría. Now this basin with its scattered, broad-crowned Canary palms and terraced fields forms the island's green heart. But the Famaras are also of volcanic origin, and here, alongside the 2000 ft Monte Corona, you will see the

Photo: Cueva de los Verdes

Caves and fields, lava rocks and craters, beaches and cliffs – nowhere else on the island is as colourful and varied

island's most impressive craters. When there was a volcanic eruption in 3000 BC – long before the island was settled – the Jameos del Agua and the Cueva de los Verdes were created. These two amazing cave systems are well worth exploring.

Alongside the coast road to Órzola is the Malpaís de la Corona, the 'badlands' of the Corona volcano. The sombre lunar landscape of sharp-edged magma clumps is even now, some 5000 years after its formation, of no agricultural value. Light green moss is the only form of vegetation on the lava-strewn wasteland, while tough tabaiba bushes with finger-thick branches have thrust their roots deep into the cracks. Given the inhospitable terrain, it is all the more remarkable that there are so many beaches of fine golden sand on this part of the coast. It's hard to resist stopping and taking a dip. Finally you reach the fishing village of Órzola, renowned for its bars and restaurants. Ferries to the island of La Graciosa leave from here.

Costa Teguise: white houses, black mountains and Atlantic waves

COSTA TEGUISE

(125 D–E4) *(₥ G 9)* **Twenty years ago anyone keeping a close eye on the island's development would have expected Costa Teguise to be the place with the fastest development.**
The developed plots of land that extend deep inland show clearly just how ambitious the original plans were. But since building work came to a standstill in 1990, calm has returned and the authorities in Teguise are now pursuing a more leisurely development plan. As a result the holiday experience in the tourist villages north of the island's capital is gentler than in lively Puerto del Carmen. Despite that the hotels here are reckoned to be the best in the Canaries, the five-star *Gran Meliá Salinas* being a fine example. Two other projects bear the unmistakeable signature of César Manrique: the *Pueblo Marinero* – the mariners' village –

a pretty complex of several blocks around inner courtyards and the *Villa La Mareta*, which can only be viewed from a distance. The magnificent estate was built by King Hussein of Jordan, who later presented it as a gift to the Spanish king, Juan Carlos I. Now this closely guarded mareta is used solely as a hideaway for the royal family, the president and foreign guests.

FOOD & DRINK

The trade winds that blow along Costa Teguise's coastal strip have always been a source of irritation for restaurant waiters. Much of their time was spent chasing flying table cloths. To prevent this many restaurant terraces are protected from the wind or glazed with panoramic screens, so that waiting staff can get on with their work– and diners don't have to keep removing sand from their food and teeth.

CASA BLANCA
Lovely food and an atmosphere to match. Fresh fish and succulent South American

steaks are cooked over an open fire, which is visible to guests in the dining area. *Closed at lunch time | Calle Las Olas 4 | tel. 928 59 01 55 | Expensive*

HELGA'S PASTELERÍA
Hidden well away in the Pueblo Marinero and with a hint of romance – a German master baker is behind the appetising array of tarts, tartlets, cakes, pastries and nibbles on sale in this pâtisserie. Sit on the terrace and enjoy the view of a huge fig tree. *Daily | Plaza del Pueblo Marinero 8 | www.helgas-pasteleria.com | Budget*

ISLA BONITA ● ⏱
Señor Pepe only buys from local farmers, as he knows that fresh ingredients taste best. Specialities include mild onions grown in lava trenches, sweet tomatoes and water melons, origin-protected lentils *(lentejas de Lanzarote)*, goat's cheese at all stages of maturity, kid and sucking pig. Then there's the fresh catch from Arrecife's fishing fleet. The recipes are traditional Lanzarote dishes, spiced up and seasoned to perfection. Almost all of the wine is from the island. Give the organic wine from Bodega Bermejo a try. Popular with the locals, above-average price bracket *Closed Sun | Avda. del Mar s/n | tel. 928 59 15 26 | Moderate*

EL PESCADOR
Good, down-to-earth Canarian and international cuisine in the relaxing setting of Manrique's mariners' village. *Closed Sun and lunch time | Plaza del Pueblo Marinero | tel. 928 59 08 74 | Moderate*

INSIDER TIP REPIKADA
This is where you will find Lanzarote's best tapas – and nothing else. No menu, trust your eyes, select at the counter and enjoy. *Closed Tue | Avda Islas Canarias | tel. 928 34 68 67 | Budget–Moderate*

VILLA TOLEDO
Restaurant with terrace right on the seafront above rocks. Good fish and meat menu. *Daily | Avda Los Cocederos s/n | tel. 928 59 06 26 | Moderate*

WINDSURFING CLUB
The shop at the southern end of Playa de las Cucharas sells or rents out first-rate branded windsurfing equipment. *Calle Las Olas 18*

SHOPPING

LA TIERRA
Pretty, colourful pottery items of decent quality. Manrique's Timanfaya Devil available in five sizes. *Plaza del Pueblo Marinero*

MERCADILLO
The Pueblo Marinero is the atmospheric backdrop to the Friday evening market (from 5pm): Artisans from all over the island sell lava jewellery and watercolours with Lanzarote motifs, fabrics and pottery.

LOW BUDGET

▶ The Aparthotel Lanzarote Bay, fully refurbished in 2008, beats all prices in Costa Teguise. Some 200 villas clustered around the pool area; the price starts at 54 euros per day for a double room. *Avda Las Palmeras 30 | tel. 928 59 02 46*

▶ If you want to admire the stunning view of La Graciosa at the *Mirador del Río* without paying the admission fee, get close to the cliff top some 200 m from the road.

▶ Prices in the *Los Pescaditos* fish restaurant in Arrieta with a small terrace overlooking the coast are very low. Most dishes cost less than 7 euros. *Closed Tue | tel. 928 84 82 66*

ENTERTAINMENT

Only at the weekend do the clubs and bars fill up. The nightlife is aimed primarily at British tourists. There's often live music in The Snug in the Pueblo Marinero. It's a bit quieter in the Orient Express, while the Hook with pirate decor prefers pop and rock music.

INSIDER TIP ▶ **JAZZ MI MADRE!**
This place attracts followers of jazz and similar like bees to a honeypot. Especially on one of the three days in the week when there are live acts on the small stage. *Mon–Sat from 10pm | Avda Islas Canaris, opposite Pueblo Marinero*

WHERE TO STAY

BARCELÓ LA GALEA
Small, compact apartment hotel near Playa de las Cucharas with a pool and professional animation team. The rooms near the pool can be quite noisy. *156 rooms | Plaza Montaña Clara | tel. 928 59 05 51 | www.barcelolagalea.com | Moderate*

GRAN MELIÁ SALINAS
The amazing pool zone in the Canary Islands' best-known hotel was designed by César Manrique; his idea of filling out the inner area with luxuriant gardens pointed the way for holiday hotels all over the world. When it opened in 1977, it was chosen as one of the ten most beautiful hotels in the world. Two decades later, it was time was for a facelift. Two restaurants and a spa were included

in the plans, and nine exclusive garden villas were added; the largest has its own swimming pool. *310 rooms | Avda Islas Canarias | tel. 928 59 00 40 | www.solme lia.com | Expensive*

LANZAROTE GARDENS
This quiet, family-friendly apartment hotel complex is a five-minute walk from the beach, but is beginning to show its age. Some 242 apartments are clustered around a leafy garden with children's pool and a well-equipped playground. *Avda Islas Canarias 13 | tel. 928 59 01 00 | www.h10hotels.com | Moderate*

OCCIDENTAL GRAND TEGUISE PLAYA
The most impressive feature here is the extravagantly planted, multi-storey indoor plaza, ringed by galleries, from which 314 rooms can be reached. There's a circular bar right in the middle. This large hotel has several pools and also direct access to the Playa del Jablillo. *Avda del Jablillo | tel. 928 59 06 54 | www. occidental-hoteles.com | Expensive*

INFORMATION

TOURIST OFFICE
Avda Islas Canarias/Pueblo Marinero | tel. 928 59 25 42 | www.teguiseturismo.com

WHERE TO GO

ARRIETA (121 E5) (*H 6*)
This former fishing harbour has grown dramatically in the last few years. The small but pretty La Garita town beach occupies a sheltered position. For sightseers the only place of interest in the town is the *Casa Juanita*, known as the Blue House or *Casa Azul*. An impressive structure, it was built beside the sea by a lanzaroteño who had amassed a fortune in Venezuela. The deep blue upper façade

Delicious with a glass of white wine: fish in El Charcón in Arrieta

and red bricks below contrast with the plain, white traditional low-rise houses in the village. A bold design at the time it was built, today it's a slightly odd mix of styles and colours.

The fish restaurants in Arrieta enjoy a fine reputation. *El Pisquito (daily | tel. 6 60 46 51 06 | Moderate)* sits by the water. Situated on the mole, equipped with a large ship's telescope and offering a view of the Blue House is *El Charcón (closed Wed | tel. 928 84 81 10 | www.elcharcon.com | Moderate)*, where Señor Ricardo, the owner, happily dispenses the La Grieta house wine. His white wine, and the rather rare, for Lanzarote, red have designation of origin status. Always popular is a visit to *Amanecer (closed Thu | La Garita 46 | tel. 928 83 54 84 | Moderate)*, where a team of brothers cook freshly caught

A magical world: César Manrique's Jardín de Cactus

behind galleries and caverns at various levels, which together reach a height of 40 m and extend far out into the sea.

At the time of the pirate attacks the Cueva de los Verdes served as a refuge, as it was well hidden. In 1618, however, Algerian buccaneers discovered the caves through an act of betrayal and carried off hundreds of people into slavery.

The guided tour through this bizarre underworld inside the lava lasts 45 minutes and covers a distance of over a mile. Subtle lighting and esoteric music transform the walk into a dream sequence. Halfway along there's a large auditorium where everyone can take a rest. At the end, there's another special effect, but we won't spoil the experience by giving away details. *Daily 10am–5pm | admission 8 euros (including guided tour)*. Concerts are held in the auditorium. Enquire if any are imminent, because they are memorable occasions (*www.centrosturisticos.com*).

GUATIZA (125 E2) (*ⱷ G–H 7*)

Fields of cacti as far as the eye can see. Every open space in and around Guatiza is planted with the fleshy opuntia cactus. Farmers with low-fitting straw hats pass along the rows. An avenue of old eucalyptus trees runs through the village, which was once prosperous courtesy of the cochineal beetle. Although the trade in natural dyes is now over, between Guatiza and Mala the tiny creatures are still painstakingly harvested.

At the entrance to the village, the road branches off to the right to Los Cocoteros and one of Lanzarote's last functioning salt ponds. The **INSIDERTIP** *Salina Los Cocoteros* is easy to spot as it still uses wind-powered pumps. Seawater is left to evaporate in hundreds of ponds, and as the water disappears, it leaves behind a thick layer of fine salt grains.

The ★ *Jardín de Cactus* at the end of the

fish without frills, but very well. Right on the playa at the ● **INSIDERTIP** *Chiringo Beach* bar (*daily | Budget*), tapas, sandwiches, paella and milkshakes are served to the accompaniment of cool jazz music. For something a little more upmarket, pay a visit to **INSIDERTIP** *El Marinero* (*tel. 6 20 211 8 62 | Moderate*), where by appointment (ideally the day before, as the day when the restaurant is closed changes) a delicious *menú de degustación* is served.

CUEVA DE LOS VERDES ★
(121 E5) (*ⱷ H 6*)

The Cueva de los Verdes is part of a 4.5-mile lava tunnel, the Túnel de la Atlántida. The cave was formed when Monte Corona erupted 5000 years ago. Streams of lava, which at the time flowed into the sea, quickly cooled down at the surface, while the hot magma beneath continued on its course. When the eruptions stopped, the residues flowed out, leaving

village is devoted to the spiny world of cacti. César Manrique collected 1420 different types of cactus in the broad pit of a former quarry at the foot of a restored gofio mill. The cactus garden was his final task. Fragments of black lava and high stone columns add to this bizarre setting, so it is not surprising visitors imagine themselves lost in an alien world. A restaurant here serves traditional food and drinks and a shop sells souvenirs. *Daily 10am–5.45pm | admission 5 euros*

JAMEOS DEL AGUA ★
(121 F5) (*ₒₒ H 6*)

Like the Cueva de los Verdes, the Jameos del Agua is part of the Atlántida tunnel system. Until the late 1960s farmers deposited refuse through two gaping holes (jameos) in the lava blanket. We owe a debt of gratitude to César Manrique for clearing out and saving the *jameos*. He retained the structure of this natural phenomenon, but transformed it into a magical work of art. Visitors descend through a wide funnel, whose walls are overgrown with subtropical plants. If you eat in the terraced restaurant, you can admire the view over an enchanting salt-water lake, home to a species of white crab. As the creatures survive in the dark, they have no sight. Do not throw coins into the water, as they are susceptible to metal oxide.

Behind the lake, where visitors stop and stare, Manrique created a dazzling white pool with water shimmering turquoise in the glaring sunlight, which enters through a second hole in the lava covering. In the next lava tube there is an auditorium boasting superb acoustics. Concerts, sometimes by folk music groups, are staged here. *Daily 10am–6pm (admission 8 euros), Tue, Fri and also Sat 7pm–2am (with folk music, admission 9 euros) | www.centrosturisticos.com*

Idyllic: the swimming pool at the exit of the Jameos del Agua cave

Living in lava:
Manrique's home

and public holidays from 2pm, when the locals arrive, a band plays Canarian and Cuban folk ballads. But people don't just come to Órzola to eat. Almost every hour, little boats shuttle between the port and the island of La Graciosa.

There are a number of fine beaches nearby. The spectacular *Playa de la Cantería* beneath the towering Famara Mountains can be reached as part of a walk. Southwest of Órzola, only a few metres from the LZ-1, there are more magnificent playas to explore, such as the ● sandy beaches at Caletón Blanco. Note here the striking contrast between the black lava rocks and the almost snow-white sand. Because the water in the sheltered bays is shallow, the sea is several degrees warmer than elsewhere and suitable for young children.

TABAYESCO (121 E6) *(𝄞 G 6)*

Tabayesco nestles amid steeply climbing terraced fields dedicated to the cultivation of vegetables and by the mouth of the fertile ↙ Valle de Temisa. Among the crops grown by the villagers in their gardens are avocado pears, almonds, oranges and, unusually for Lanzarote, bananas. A winding road leads up into the Famara Mountains.

ÓRZOLA (121 E3) *(𝄞 H 4)*

The small fishing port in the far north of the island is definitely worth a visit, if only to watch ferocious surf crashing against the rocks. There are a number of rustic-style fish restaurants here. The ocean's harvest is served fresh in the *Charco Viejo (closed Mon | Calle La Quemadita 8 | tel. 928 84 25 91 | Moderate)* and in the *Perla del Atlántico (closed Mon | Calle Peña San Dionisio 1 | tel. 928 84 25 89 | Moderate)*. Señor Antonio in the **INSIDER TIP** *Os Gallegos (daily | Calle La Quemadita 6 | tel. 928 84 25 02 | Moderate)* serves up some generous fish platters. On Sunday

TAHICHE (125 D4) *(𝄞 F 8–9)*

Visitors to Lanzarote keen on gaining a better understanding of the visions and the achievements of the island's greatest artist will almost certainly want to pay a visit to the ★ *Fundación César Manrique* in Tahiche. The foundation occupies the artist's former home, which is situated near a roundabout showcasing a large Manrique mobile made from stainless steel. A large part of César Manrique's oeuvre and also pieces by his artist friends are exhibited here, but the extraordinary house alone is worth a visit.

One remarkable feature is the section of the futuristic underground lounge built into lava bubbles. *Winter Mon–Sat 10am–6pm, Sun 10am–3pm, Summer daily 10am–7pm | admission 8 euros | www.fcmanrique.org*

YÉ (121 E4) (*ⓜ G 5*)

The village of Yé clings to the mountainside at a height of around 1300 ft beneath the impressive panorama of the eroded Monte Corona, whose ragged crater edge bears a remarkable similarity to a crown (corona). When arriving from Arrieta, just before the village, you will pass the former La Torrecilla del Domingo vineyard, whose name is a reference to the striking 'mini-tower', which can be seen from some distance. The *Volcán de la Corona* restaurant *(closed Monday | tel. 928 52 65 16 | Moderate)* near the junction serves fresh food straight from the charcoal grill.

ISLA GRACIOSA

(120 121 C–E 1–3) (*ⓜ F–G 3–4*) ★ **Anyone wishing to make the crossing from Órzola to the tiny island of La Graciosa needs good sea legs.** During the first ten minutes of the journey the small boats are buffeted by the high waves of the untamed Atlantic Ocean.

But once into the El Río straits the waves usually subside and the waters become much calmer. And that tranquillity continues on land. This island is a thoroughly agreeable relic from the past. Before the advent of tourism to the Canaries, this was what life was like on the islands – or at least very similar. The main village of *Caleta del Sebo* (121 D3) (*ⓜ G 4*) consists of a few plain houses and a tiny maze of streets, none of them made up. There are only a few 4 x 4 vehicles

on La Graciosa. But time has not left everything unscathed. There are a few restaurants, which cater for the needs of the many day-trippers. Practically every house has apartments to let, there is a well-stocked supermarket and even a disco. But in the end none of this has very much to do with mass tourism Lanzarote-style, so one quickly senses that the emphasis here is on old-fashioned recreational pursuits. The *Playa de Francesa*, the *Playa de la Cocina* and, above all, the ● INSIDER TIP *Playa de las Conchas* in the north rank among the finest and most isolated beaches in the Canaries. So La Graciosa continues to be an island haven reserved for a few beach joggers, walkers, bird-watchers and lovers of peace and quiet – at least for the time being. What is certain is that the other, even smaller islands in the Chinijo archipelago will remain unspoilt for a very long time to come. *Alegranza* and *Montaña Clara* are not just protected nature reserves, but also much too wild and too remote. There is, however, a water taxi which does a circuit of the islands, so that they can at least be seen from the coast. *Passenger ferries (no vehicle transport) of Líneas Marítimas Romero daily from Órzola at 10am, 11am, noon, 1.30pm, 4pm, 5pm and 6pm, from La Graciosa at 8am, 10am, 11am, 12.30pm, 3pm, 4pm and 5pm | return crossing 20 euros | tel. 9 02 40 16 66 | www.lineas-romero.com*

FOOD & DRINK

The two pensiones mentioned below have basic, but good restaurants *(Budget)* on their ground floor. Also worth recommending is the *El Marinero (Calle García Escamez 11)* near the church, which is run by the ever-present Romero family – most of the ferries also belong to this clan. Rather more up-to-date and more expensive is *El Varadero* (*Moderate*), which is right by the ferry pier. A little further on into the village by the harbour basin is the *El Chiringuito bar*. This is the meeting place for the locals, the fishing community and anyone else in need of a relaxed chat.

WHERE TO STAY

PENSION ENRIQUETA
This pension in the centre of the village can offer eight basic rooms with bathroom. *Calle Barlovento 6 | tel. 928 84 20 51 | Budget*

PENSION GIRASOL PLAYA
Now it has been renovated, the 'sunflower' is much more comfortable than in the past. It has rooms and also brand new apartments in the annex, most of them with a fine harbour view. *Calle García Escamez 1 | tel. 928 84 21 18 | www. graciosaonline.com | Budget*

WALKS

There is a wide selection of walks to choose from on La Graciosa. Walk-

ers who consider themselves to be in good shape could climb either of the following volcanoes from its less steep side: the ☀ *Montaña del Mojón* (121 D2–3) (*Ⓜ G 4*) in the middle of the island and the ☀ *Montaña Bermeja* (121 D1–2) (*Ⓜ G 3*) in the north. But the island is too large to get round all in one

LIVING ON THE LAND: TURISMO RURAL

☺ Spending time living on the land like the lanzaroteños makes for a very special holiday experience. The type of accommodation offered can range from comfortable, fully furnished modern apartments for self-caterers to country villas with all services provided. They will usually be well away from the main tourist centres and are ideal for families. What is more, you will be staying not in some vast villa complex, but in a traditional, centuries-old house, helping to sustain local architecture and communities. Rates for turismo rural accommodation are often well below those for conventional hotels. Rental periods are often on a weekly, but can also be on a day basis. Because most are in remote locations, a hire car is essential. For further information and reservations: *www.lanzarote-finca.com, www.ecoturismocanarias.com, www.real-lanzarote.com, www.holidaylettings.co.uk*

There's always another volcanic cone in the way: walkers on the Isla Graciosa

day. Some walkers may prefer to join a guided tour, in which case they can call on the services of ☺ *Explora La Graciosa*. Eva Maldener, who has lived on the island for more than a decade, offers walks focussing on La Graciosa's flora – choose a half-day or a whole day walk. She will also help out if you are looking for accommodation on the island *(Calle Popa 15 | Caleta del Sebo | tel. 928 84 21 94 | exploralagraciosa@gmx.net)*.

The two varied circular walks described below may be undertaken independently. Neither is too strenuous.

INSIDER TIP ▶ NORTHERN ROUTE

A track leads through the middle of the island from Caleta del Sebo (121 D3) *(𝓜 G 4)* and between the two volcanic cones of the Montaña del Mojón and the Agujas Grandes and then through to the *Playa de las Conchas* (121 D1–2) *(𝓜 G 3)*. This beach must be one of the finest on the Canary Islands. But take care if you feel inclined to take a

dip. Because of the strong waves and currents the waters here are dangerous even for experienced swimmers. Below the Montaña Bermeja turn towards the north coast to reach the spectacular dunes near *Playa Lambra* (121 D–E1) *(𝓜 G 3)*. You can't miss the astonishing sight of countless millions of shells, in places completely covering the surface of the sand. Return to the harbour at Caleta via the village of *Pedro Barba* (121 E2) *(𝓜 G 4)*, which is not permanently inhabited. *Approx. 10 mi or 4 hours*

SOUTHERN ROUTE

If you choose the southern route, leave Caleta along the harbour basin. When you reach the pretty *Playa del Salado* (121 D3) *(𝓜 G 4)*, look out for a track, which you should follow. If walking in the hot sun, it's worth going a little further south for two even more beautiful beaches, the *Playa Francesa* (121 C–D3) *(𝓜 G 4)* and the *Playa de la Cocina* (120 C3) *(𝓜 F 4–5)*. Now return a short distance and on the shore side pass below the *Montaña Amarilla*, the 'yellow mountain', to reach the west coast. There you will join a track, which first passes vegetable fields and then, keeping the Montaña del Mojón always on the right-hand side, return to Caleta. *Approx. 6 mi or 2.5 hours*

WHERE TO GO

ALEGRANZA (0) (*M G 1*)

This inhospitable island of 4.5 square miles is no longer inhabited. Like the whole archipelago, it is now a nature conservation area. The marine life here is unspoilt and varied, and many rare bird species nest on the island. La Graciosa's smaller neighbouring island is not open to visitors, but you can hire the water taxi and Dani, its pilot, and make your own tour of the spectacular coastline *(please note: Dani speaks very little English | tel.6 76 90 18 45)*. Experienced divers enjoy the challenge of exploring the underwater world of the Reserva Marina *(for further information: www.lineas-romero.com)*.

TEGUISE

(124 C2) (*M F 8*) ● **When you arrive in Teguise (pop. 17,000), it will seem as if you have made a journey back in time. You will be greeted by grand villas with high wooden portals and then have to squeeze through narrow alleyways to reach imposing churches and broad plazas.**

There is very little evidence that almost 600 years have passed since the founding of the Real Villa, the royal town of Teguise. Maciot de Béthencourt built the first colonial town on the Canary Islands in 1428, on the site of Aldea Grande, an even older Majo settlement, and named it after his wife, a Majo princess. Teguise remained the capital of the island until 1852. Powerful families, such as the Herreras and Feo Perazas, built their townhouses here.

But why up there so far from the coast? This is a good question, as cool trade winds blow through the streets, clouds often shroud the town in mist and it is always cooler than by the sea. But the early inhabitants had good reason to choose this settlement. During the winter the vital rain falling on the neighbouring mountain of Guanapay was collected in a giant underground cistern, the *Gran Mareta*. These caverns were restored in 1992, but unfortunately are no longer accessible. Furthermore, the Spanish colonials would almost certainly have felt safer away from the coast given the threat of pirate attacks. The protection offered by the powerful castle, the Castillo Santa Bárbara built nearby on the Guanapay, gave added protection.

But they were wrong. Teguise was repeatedly attacked from the sea. A plaque in the *Callejón de Sangre* (Blood Alley) behind the Church of Nuestra Señora de Guadalupe recalls a massacre carried out by the feared Algerian buccaneers in 1586. In 1618 the place was burnt the place to the ground, so the oldest surviving buildings date from the 17th century. But that doesn't take anything away from their splendour. The historic centre of the town with its unique architectural style has been under a preservation order since 1973.

Now Teguise leads a double life. On weekdays the place often looks as if it has been abandoned. Only a handful of children play on the central Plaza de la Constitución, a few women will be out shopping and small groups of men will be sitting around in bars. The town appears to exist only as a museum:

it's well-preserved and steeped in history, but lifeless. Most of the houses are empty, because the local people work in the holiday centres during the day. But on Sunday the place comes alive and almost bursts at the seams for market day. The *mercadillo* here is one of Lanzarote's main attractions. Holidaymakers arrive in their thousands; countless traders in white vans, here to peddle kitsch

as there is nothing quite so hectic and chaotic anywhere else on Lanzarote. And then by Sunday evening Teguise has returned to its slumbers.

CASTILLO SANTA BÁRBARA ☼

The small but solid fortification on the Guanapay volcano outside Teguise

Quiet time: The main plaza in Teguise with the Church of Nuestra Señora de Guadalupe

and knick-knacks from all over the world, also descend on the town. Folk groups are on hand to entertain the throngs of visitors. The streets and the squares, the whole town in fact, resembles an oriental bazaar. In the bars shoppers jostle for drinks, which are often much dearer than elsewhere on the island. The Gran Mareta, the rather forlorn plaza above the ancient cisterns behind the church, is jam-packed with takeaway food stalls. Although all the bustle has very little to do with day-to-day life on the island, the *mercadillo* is something to behold,

is visible from some distance. It can be reached via a tarmac road, which branches off to the right to Haría at the north end of the town. This fortress was built in the 16th century to protect the islanders from pirate attacks. Sometimes thousands of frightened islanders sought refuge within its walls.

The entrance is a separate stone staircase with drawbridge. Santa Bárbara was fully restored in the 1970s and 1980s. Initially a museum documenting emigration from the Canary Islands was housed there, but with the recent re-emergence

Convento de San Francisco: a church and also a venue for exhibiting sacred woodcarvings

of piracy on the high seas, it was decided to explore this topic, and the castle has become the International Pirate Museum featuring exhibits on the numerous attacks Lanzarote endured at the hands of pirates from across Africa and Europe *(Sun–Fri 10am–3pm | admission 3 euros)*. Do take the opportunity to go up onto the roof for a magnificent view over the northern half of the island.

LA CILLA

This former tithe house, built in the 17th century, was the collecting point for the corn tax, which Lanzarote was expected to pay to the bishop on Gran Canaria. Now it houses a branch of the Canarian savings bank. *Mon–Fri 8am–2pm, Thu also 5.30–7.30pm*

CONVENTO DE SAN FRANCISCO

The former convent church, typically for the Canary Islands, has aisles of different lengths. It is home to an interesting collection of sacred woodcarvings and a skilfully carved timber ceiling in mudéjar style. *Irregular opening, most likely Sun | admission 2 euros*

CONVENTO DE SANTO DOMINGO

Changing exhibitions of modern Canarian art, an interesting contrast to the old nave, are now staged in the church of the Dominican monastery (founded 1726). *Sun–Fri 10am–3pm | admission 1.50 euros*

GRAN MARETA

This cistern, once the largest on Lanzarote, was built to store rainwater. Later it silted up. When the desalination plants were commissioned, it was surplus to requirements and was concreted over. Now the broad plaza behind the church is used to stage outdoor events and as space for the Sunday market.

IGLESIA DE NUESTRA SEÑORA DE GUADALUPE

This parish church on the Plaza de la Constitución was consecrated in the 15th century, destroyed by pirates in 1680, then subsequently rebuilt. It is dedicated to Our Lady of Guadalupe, who is revered in Spain and in South America. The impressive façade with its huge stone tower contributes to the relaxed atmosphere on the plaza. After a fire in 1909, it was restored in neo-Gothic style, but this did little to improve the interior of the church.

PALACIO MARQUÉS DE HERRERA Y ROJAS

This rather nondescript palace (1455) has a fine, covered inner courtyard. An exhibition of pieces made by the local craft school occupies the vestibule. Admission is free, but not all the rooms are open to the public. *Mon–Fri 8am–3pm | Calle José Betancort*

PALACIO DE SPÍNOLA ●

The prized gem in old Teguise is the Spínola Palace on the plaza. It was built between 1730 and 1780 by the nobleman and politician José Feo Peraza and was the residence for the governor of Lanzarote throughout the 18th century. All the furnishings have survived remarkably well. Particularly impressive is the extravagant use of hardwoods on the sturdy portals and the solid, sealed wooden flooring. The patio with fountain and overhanging bougainvillea are also pretty; the dining table is always set in grand style, as if an important visitor is about to arrive. At the rear of the palacio is the kitchen with an open fireplace and the two-metre-wide hearth. Adjoining it is another inner courtyard with palm trees and an old fig tree. *Mon–Fri 9am–4pm, Sun 10am–3pm | admission 3 euros*

PLAZA DE LA CONSTITUCIÓN ★

Around the central square in Teguise with its palm and laurel trees are some of the finest examples of Lanzarote's colonial architecture. Between the former La Cilla grain store and the church sit two lions gazing intently at the 18th-century Palacio de Spínola.

FOOD & DRINK

ACATIFE

A classic among Lanzarote's restaurants in a venerable building. Traditional, but outstanding fare – at prices to match. Try the rabbit in red wine sauce *(conejo al vino tinto)*! *Closed Mon | Calle San Miguel 4 | tel. 928 84 50 37 | Moderate*

BODEGA SANTA BÁRBARA

Wine and snacks served in the mini-patio of this small bodega, inside more dishes. A mouth-watering range of tapas in the display cabinet. *Closed Sat | Calle La Cruz s/n | tel. 928 59 48 41 | Moderate*

CASA LEÓN / HESPÉRIDES ☺

Located in an old townhouse, this small restaurant serves tasty homemade cakes and vegetarian dishes. Much of it comes from the organic shop next door. Very reasonable prices given the quality! *Daily | Calle León y Castillo 3 | tel. 928 59 40 12 | www.biohesperides.blog spot.com | Moderate*

PATIO DEL VINO

The owner of the old Palacio del Marqués spent a lot of money on restoration work and opened a top-class patio restaurant here. By special request groups can ask for VIP treatment and receive attentive service in a small circle. The proprietor is proud of his well-stocked cellar. *Closed evenings and Sat | Calle Herrera y Rojas 9 | tel. 928 84 57 73 | www.patiodelvino. com | Expensive*

LA TAHONA

The menu in this restaurant beside the Convento de Santo Domingo features traditional Canarian dishes, such as *sancocho* (fish) and *ropa vieja* (stew). Very popular with the locals – always a good sign! On Sunday guests like to reach for then it probably doesn't exist – everything from art and arty knickknacks to day-to-day items such as second-hand clothing, shoes and fresh fruit. Also on sale are

Party-time Lanzarote-style: music-makers love to return to their Canarian roots in La Tahona restaurant

a guitar or timple and sing traditional songs. *Daily | Calle Santo Domingo 3 | tel. 928 84 58 92 | Moderate*

SHOPPING

Teguise has always been an important centre of Canarian culture. And in recent years more and more artists and artisans from northern Europe have moved to the island. The town's shops stock a large selection of crafts, jewellery and paintings.

LA LONJA EXCLUSIVA
This small shop sells approved copies of works by César Manrique. *Plaza de 18 de Julio*

MERCADILLO
The large Sunday market is the perfect place for browsers. If you can't find it here,

many delicious forms of farm produce: *chorizo*, the piquant pork sausage with dried red peppers, or *turrón*, a nougat dessert in many different variations. *Sun 9am–2pm | buses leave from the holiday centres and Arrecife, charges payable for parking on the edge of the town*

TIMPLES ●
Antonio Lemes Hernández is one of the last craftsmen making the famous Canarian guitar. For almost all his life he has been in his workshop piecing together the parts for about 15 different instruments of varying sizes, from the mini-timple to the contra-timple. A beautiful but expensive souvenir. The standard instrument costs around 200 euros, more elaborate models with pearl inlays and marquetry 400–500 euros. *Calle Flores 8*

WHERE TO STAY

INSIDER TIP FINCA MALVARROSA

Former farmhouse with two apartments within easy walking distance from the centre. Both are furnished attractively in rustic style. Amenities include kitchen, bathroom, terrace and swimming pool. *Calle Malvarrosa 41 | tel. 928 59 30 17 | www.fincamalvarrosa.com | Moderate*

INFORMATION

TOURIST OFFICE

With audioguides. *Plaza de la Constitución | tel. 928 84 53 98 | www.teguiseturismo.com*

WHERE TO GO

ERMITA DE LAS NIEVES ☼
(125 D1) (*Ø* F–G 7)

This whitewashed pilgrimage chapel, literally the Hermitage of the Snow, stands high up on the Risco de Famara. The chapel is dedicated to the Virgen de las Nievas or Our Lady of the Snows, who has over the years received countless pleas for rain to fall on Lanzarote. Although the chapel is usually closed, the long climb is worth the effort, if only to see one of the **INSIDER TIP** finest panoramic views on the island. The cliffs drop almost vertically 1960 ft into the sea. The islands of La Graciosa and Montaña Clara, the Playa de Famara, Teguise and the Timanfaya volcano are clearly visible. Access above the wind turbine farm on the left

HARÍA ★ **(121 D5) (*Ø* G 6)**

When suddenly you descend into the valley of a thousand palms at the foot of the Famara Mountains, the scene is more Africa than Europe. Countless broad-crowned Canarian palms stand proudly among the low, white houses.

Haría (pop. 5000) is the friendliest place on Lanzarote. It is where you will see how lanzaroteños used to live. So no surprise then that in his old age César Manrique retired to Haría and is buried here.

Take a stroll through the village to discover old villas with luxuriant patios, small shops and bars. The *Plaza León y Castillo* with its shady weeping fig trees opens out in front of the church and is the perfect place for a break. The small *Museo Sacro Popular* in an old but pretty house on the square near the church displays sacred sculptures and paintings, but it is only open during the Saturday market.

Women gather in the *Taller Municipal de Artesanía* craft centre *(summer Mon–Sat 10am–1pm and 3pm–5pm, winter 10am–3pm and 4pm–6pm)* near the Plaza de la Constitución to work on embroidery and shawls in keeping with the old tradition. If you would like to see Don Eulogio, the last basket weaver on Lanzarote, at work, call in and ask the way. These labour-intensive goods are sold on the **INSIDER TIP** *Saturday market (mercadillo)* and you will see many more artisans selling their wares here too. Also on sale here are home-made speciality food and drinks, e.g. ☺ organic goat's cheese from Haría. You will quickly see that not all market traders are native Lanzaroteans.

Temporary exhibitions are held in the *El Aljibe* gallery *(Mon–Sat 10am–3pm)*, formerly the water reservoir beneath the plaza. You can eat Canarian-style in *Dos Hermanos (daily | tel. 928 83 54 09 | Moderate)*. Come here if you would like to sample some goat specialities, but do check the price before ordering. The *Cafeteria Ney-Ya* is loud and lively *(daily | Budget)* – between Haría's two plazas.

Omar Sharif once lazed around beneath these palm trees here: LagOmar

MIRADOR DE GUINATE ● ☼
(121 D4) (*Ø G 5*)

The view from the Mirador de Guinate near the village of the same name is no less spectacular than the view from the Mirador del Río – but free. On the way there you pass the Tropical Parque, which is great fun and not just for children.

MIRADOR DEL RÍO ★ ☼
(121 E3) (*Ø G 4–5*)

Stunning is the only word to describe the view from this fortification, the Batería del Río, perched precariously on a cliff top at a height of 1570 ft in the far north of Lanzarote. The view extends as far as the islands of La Graciosa and Alegranza. Dating from 1974, the mirador complex was one of César Manrique's first works.

As you would expect from a man dedicated to preserving Lanzarote's heritage, it fits perfectly into the environment. *Daily 10am–5.45pm | admission 4.50 euros*

NAZARET (124–125 C–D3) (*Ø F 8*)

Hidden away in a former quarry is this eccentric, fortress-like estate. The complex, which today bears the name **INSIDERTIP** *LagOmar*, was built in the 1970s, before Lanzarote had appeared in any holiday brochures. Its first owner was the actor Omar Sharif, of Dr Zhivago fame, who it is said gambled it away in a game of bridge.

Now the place is a 'museum'. You can walk through caves and tunnels, set at different levels around an artificial lake, as you pass the Sharif Room. On display here are posters recalling the great actor's heyday; there is even a photo of that fateful card game. During the day, the café-restaurant serves tapas and dishes of the day, but in the evening it's more high-class Mediterranean-style dining. The cave bar in lounge style *(Chillout-Bar La Cueva: closed Mon | Ap. Casa Sharif | tel. 928 84 54 60 | Expensive)* is perfect for upmarket relaxation. Magical evenings at Bar La Cueva begin at 8pm, when the volcanic rocks are transformed into deep red, with candles and subtle lighting creating a special ambience. Try a mojito or a daiquirí! In addition, set into the rock are two apartments with modern furnishings. Amenities include a terrace and pool, plus an expansive view over Lanzarote's central plain. *Museo & Restaurant LagOmar: closed Monday | Calle Los Loros 6 | tel. 928 84 56 65 | www.lag-o-mar.com | admission 5 euros | Budget–Moderate*

PLAYA DE FAMARA ☼
(120–121 C–D5–6) (*Ø F–G 6*)

Famara beach is the longest on Lanzarote and scenically one of the finest.

It runs below the rugged Famara Mountains, bordered on one side by dunes and on the other by the crashing waves of the Atlantic. There's often a strong wind blowing, so pay attention to the beach safety flag. If it's red, it means positively no swimming. Every year the dangerous currents claim lives.

The *Playa Famara* villa complex may have lost some of its initial sheen, but it does occupy a stunning location on the mountainside. *50 apartments | reception open Mon–Fri 10am–noon and 5pm–7pm | tel. 928 84 51 32 | www.bungalows playafamara.com | Moderate*

A popular spot for surfers and a hideaway for those wishing to shun mass tourism is *La Caleta* (120 C 6) (*∅ F 6*). There are several bars and restaurants here. Surfers often take breakfast in the *Croissantería (daily | Budget)*. *Casa García (closed Monday | Avda El Marinero 1, on the left on the edge of the village | tel. 928 52 85 76 | Moderate)* with its green and leafy dining room is highly recommended. For the best view, try the Restaurant *El Risco (closed Mon | Calle Montaña Clara 36 | tel. 928 52 85 50 | www.restauranteelrisco.com | Moderate)*, which once belonged to a brother of César Manrique. It is now in the hands of a different proprietor and has been smartened up. What remains is the blue and white paint, the magnificent panorama of the Famara cliffs and the ever-present sound of the crashing ocean waves as a background to the chatter of guests sitting on terrace. There's a webcam so you can look the place over before dining and also check the weather.

Relaxing days on the beach with a rugged backdrop: Playa de Famara

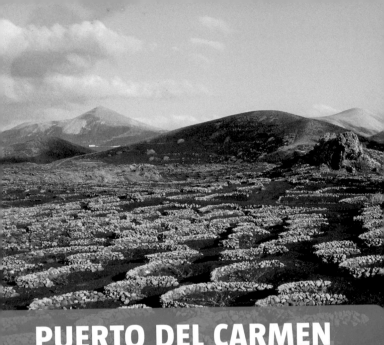

PUERTO DEL CARMEN AND THE CENTRE

The bright green vine grows in a pit about 2 metres deep, surrounded by a layered, semi-circular wall of grey stone. The soil is black, and the green leaves stand out starkly against the dark background; the vine could almost be a cheap plastic imitation.

But this is not some crazy idea dreamed up by a small-scale gardener; what you see is skilfully worked farmland on which grapes are grown commercially. Thousands of vines, each with its own small crater, cower under the harsh conditions, a dry stone wall offering scant protection. The vine-growing region extends across this lowland strip like a work by a graphic designer; it's so unreal that the New York Museum of Modern Art devoted a special exhibition to this bizarre landscape. But

can the farmers get the vines to grow using such unusual methods?

Yes, they can and it's actually very successful. To ripen the grapes in this dust-dry climate with its strong trade winds, countless tiny grains of lava – for that is what the soil consists of – are essential components. Being porous, the lapilli, as they are known, absorb moisture from the onshore wind which at night blows over La Geria – the word means windbreak – and then during the day the accumulated water gradually drips down into the roots of the vines. Only using this unique form of cultivation is it possible to bring the fruits to maturity. The result of what is known as enarenado cultivation can be seen – and sampled – between Uga and Masdache. Along the

Photo: Wine cultivation in a lava field near La Geria

The green of the vines contrasts strangely with the black soil, creating a man-made landscape that is unique on the planet

country road there are many bodegas, where the aroma of earthy wine wafts up from the cellars. The traditional Malvasia grape is now being replaced by other vine varieties, which yield a drier, lighter wine. But the wine of Lanzarote can never deny its origins. While their red wines compare poorly with those from mainland Spain, the lanzaroteños make a beautifully fresh white wine, a fine accompaniment to fish dishes and the powerful Canarian sauces.

Tourism dominates the southern coastal zone in Lanzarote's central area, particularly around Puerto del Carmen. The former farming villages of Machér, Tías and San Bartolomé have grown dramatically in recent decades and are nice enough places, but have no particular attractions. To the north of La Geria however, as far as the coast between La Santa and Sóo, old traditions linger among the people and on the land. The deliciously fruity tomatoes and the searingly hot onions, which add character to the local ensalada mixta, come from these parts.

Waiting for the next outing: boats in the harbour at Puerto del Carmen

Also grown in this part of the island is a type of baby potato which stays firm when boiled. Known as papas arrugadas, you see them on the menu in restaurants serving local specialities. They have a distinctive wrinkly skin. The region around Mancha Blanca and Tinajo is still firmly in the hands of the farming community. The fields are divided into neat plots and the green and white villages are in good shape. Tall candelabra trees (euphorbia ingens) and poinsettias grow in their carefully tended gardens. There is no mistaking the fact that tourism has brought money to the island. Until the 1970s the rural areas suffered from grinding poverty.

Happily, the receipts from tourism have played a large part in maintaining this region's cultural heritage. The church of the island's patron saint, Nuestra Señora de los Volcanes (sometimes known as Nuestra Señora de Los Dolores) has been restored to its former splendour in gleaming white. Situated on the edge

of the village of Mancha Blanca, it now welcomes visitors and the faithful. And the old farming estate, which now hosts one of the best private museums in the Canary Islands, the Museo Agrícola El Patio, would now probably be no more than an abandoned ruin.

PUERTO DEL CARMEN

MAP INSIDE THE BACK COVER
(127 F4) (*D 10*) **This former fishing village (pop. 3000) has blossomed into a top-class tourist centre. The village divides up into an older quarter around the fishing harbour and a vast expanse of holiday villages with 35,000 beds in the north.**

The main reason behind the rapid development of this small town into a major resort is the splendid beaches blessed with clean water. Now a line of bars, amusement arcades and shopping centres stretches for more than four miles along the Avenida de las Playas. This part of the town is for holidaymakers who come for the sun and to do nothing very much. If one long party on the promenade is not for you, head for the upper town or seek out one of the hotels facing away from the road. There you can enjoy your holiday undisturbed.

Puerto del Carmen has something for everyone. In the old town by the fishing harbour, the lively bustle of tourism fades into the background and the everyday life of the locals is centre-stage. Just as they have done for centuries, the fishermen will be out in the morning by their boats sorting through last night's catch. Throughout the day there always seems to be a few anglers whiling away their time on the quayside and in the evening groups of men armed with metal balls assemble for a round of pétanque. And if mass is about to start in the small chapel, Nuestra Señora del Carmen, you will find it hard to pick your way through the throng to the lively fish restaurants. Among the faithful spilling out on the street will be locals and visitors.

FOOD & DRINK

Tourist hotspot Puerto del Carmen claims to have more than 200 restaurants. But take care! Not all of them are recommended. Many, particularly along Avenida de las Playas ('The Strip'), where diners can sit with a sea view, are interested only in a rapid turnover. There is a better chance of a good meal in one of the Indian and Chinese restaurants here. If you want original Canarian dishes, perhaps with locally caught fish, it's better to look around the fishing harbour.

EL ANCLA
This new building made from red and grey volcanic blocks is just a little too flashy here, in the harbour quarter. But the tapas are always beautifully presented. Large parasols cover the terrace opposite the pétanque piste, where the men gather to enjoy their favourite pastime. *Daily | tel. 928 51 36 39 | right by the harbour | Moderate*

ANTICA TRATTORIA DI VERONA
The most popular Italian restaurant in town. The other dishes are also very tasty; friendly service. *Daily | Avda de las Playas 58 | tel. 928 51 19 53 | Moderate*

★ Jameos Playa
An enchanting hotel in Puerto del Carmen, managed to high environmental standards, designed in Canarian style and with the beach right on the doorstep → p. 67

★ La Geria
In Lanzarote's famous wine region with plenty of bodegas to choose from for tasting the local wines → p. 67

★ Casa Museo del Campesino
Farming and craft museum; watch while a souvenir of your favourite piece is custom made → p. 69

★ Museo Agrícola El Patio
The island's history lives on in Tiagua's fascinating farming museum; winner of the Canarian Culture award → p. 71

MARCO POLO HIGHLIGHTS

PUERTO DEL CARMEN

EL BODEGÓN
The top address in Puerto del Carmen, if you love tapas. *Daily | Calle Nuestra Señora del Carmen 6 | tel. 928 51 52 65 | Moderate*

INSIDER TIP ⟩ CASA ROJA ≫
On a long and narrow terrace just above the water in the old harbour basin, the perfect place for a romantic meal. There's hardly a better way of watching the sun go down. *Daily | Plaza Varadero | tel. 928 51 07 03 | Moderate*

LA LONJA
A no-nonsense meeting place for fishermen and harbour workers – with adjoining fishmonger. Plenty of tapas available from the noisy bar on the ground floor, and a large atrium brightens up the dining area on the first floor. All dishes are ultra-fresh. Try the *mero a la plancha* (grouper) and finish off the meal with a home-made *bienmesabe* with vanilla ice-cream – superb! *Daily | Calle Varadero | tel. 928 51 13 77 | Expensive*

A truly beautiful spot in the evening: the Casa Roja in Puerto del Carmen

FORTUNA ≫
The name says it all – it's in the casino, but chef José Juncal leaves nothing to chance in his award-winning kitchen. He is highly regarded for his creative dishes and the service is excellent too. You can watch the gamblers while you're eating or admire the idyllic sea view from the roof terrace. *Daily 8pm–4am | Avda de las Playas 12 | tel. 928 51 50 00 | Moderate–Expensive*

INSIDER TIP ⟩ TERRAZA PLAYA ≫
The terrace with just a handful of tables right by rocks occasionally splashed by the sea gives this restaurant a special appeal. A large menu with plenty of fish and meat dishes to choose from. *Daily | Avda de las Playas 28 | tel. 928 51 54 17 | Moderate*

SHOPPING

Plenty of cosmetics, knick-knacks and camcorders, but also an interesting range of Canary Island souvenirs. Watch out for cheap imitations of expensive brands!

CC BIOSFERA

Lots of glass and chrome went into the construction of this Centro Comercial at the western end of the town. A wide range of ladies' fashion shop competes for customers. *Avda Juan Carlos I 15*

MYSTIC

Accessories for greens and mystics: natural sponges, batik fabrics, incense. *Avda de las Playas 7*

EL NIÑO

Surf shop with a wide range of equipment from all the top brands. *Avda de las Playas, diagonally opposite the Oficina Municipal de Turismo*

BEACHES

The currents are usually weak on the beaches of Puerto del Carmen and the wind and waves moderate when the trade winds are blowing at normal strength. It's generally safe to paddle and swim and children are safe. However, the weather is not always favourable. Keep an eye on the warning notices and beach safety flags.

Basically all the beaches are equally good for bathing. The *Playa Blanca*, approx. 3/4 mile in length, was the first beach to open up to tourism. After that in an easterly direction came the *Playa de los Pocillos* and the *Playa Matagorda*, where the activity is less frenetic. The downside is that they are close to the flight path for planes arriving at Arrecife airport. The *Playa de la Barilla beach of fine sand* is especially pretty. Situated beneath the old town, it is flanked by two rocky outcrops and is the smallest and quietest of all the beaches.

LEISURE & SPORTS

Boat trips leave from the harbour in Puerto del Carmen. A return journey to Fuerteventura in the ● glass-bottomed catamaran *Princesa Icó (www.princesa-ico. com)* costs 30 euros, a day trip along the nearby coast, lunch included, costs from 45 euros. You will have to pay 44 euros for an island cruise taking in Fuerteventura and the Isla de los Lobos nature conservation area. Another option is the INSIDER TIP *Aquascope*, a submarine with windows for close-up views of underwater fauna and flora *(www.lanzarote.com/aquascope)*. A 45-minute trip costs 20 euros. Adrenaline junkies can take to the air. You are attached to both a parachute and a line on a speedboat. Before you know it, you are looking down over the beach from 650 ft *(Paracraft Lanzarote | Paseo de la Barilla | tel. 928 51 26 61 | www.lanzarote. com/paracraft | 40 euros /10 mins)*.

LOW BUDGET

▶ In Puerto del Carmen, leaflets granting free admission or discounts for theme parks or the casino are often distributed in the hotels. So keep your eyes open!

▶ Check out the basic *Pensión Magec* in the old quarter. Double rooms from 25 euros. *12 rooms | Calle Hierro 11 | tel. 928 51 51 20 | www.pension magec.com*

▶ ● Loungers on the playas in Puerto del Carmen are free from 5pm – you'll still get another two hours of sun

ENTERTAINMENT

The Avenida de las Playas, known as 'The Strip', is at the heart of Lanzarote's entertainment quarter.

AMERICAN INDIAN CAFÉ

Disco bar for 30- to 50-year-olds with live shows and video clips on screens. *Daily from 10pm | Avda. de la Playas s/n*

CASINO

Yes, Puerto del Carmen even has a casino. The normal admission charge without discount is 3 euros. *Daily 4pm–4am | Avda de las Playas 12*

INSIDER TIP ▶ CHARLIES BAR

Proceedings at the best-known live music club in Puerto del Carmen do not start until 9.30pm, but it is open seven days of the week and two bands play each evening. Genres include rock and country, reggae and Irish folk, with an occasional celebrity among the performers! *C.C. Atlántico | Avda. de las Playas | www.charlieslanzarote.com*

GOLDEN CORNER

Situated near the casino, this evening rendezvous is a quiet place to relax and is popular among people aged 30 or over for its large selection of cocktails. *Daily from 10pm | Avda. de la Playas s/n*

EL MIRADOR ☆

Beneath the palm trees, high above the beach and with a lovely view of the sea. *Daily from 8pm | Avda. de la Playas s/n*

INSIDER TIP ▶ RUTA 66

This large disco/pub is the hottest spot in Puerto del Carmen. Opens out on to the promenade. Several bars, football on wide screens and dancing to US rock bands. *From 10pm | CC Arena Dorada | Avda. de las Playas*

TROPICAL

Next door and equally popular, but the music here is more geared towards current teenie pop. Clips running on screens. *From 10pm | Avda. de las Playas CC Arena Dorada*

The well-kept beaches at Puerto del Carmen

PUERTO DEL CARMEN AND THE CENTRE

WHERE TO STAY

LAS COSTAS
This complex right by the Playa de los Pocillos has undergone a total refit and become an extravagantly glazed, ultra-modern hotel. *187 rooms | Avda de las Playas 88 | tel. 928 51 43 46 | www.hibiscus-hotels.com | Moderate*

LOS FARIONES ♨ ☺
An inviting hotel fully deserving four stars, with an extremely quiet and yet central location, a shady garden and a fine view of the Atlantic. Thanks to its recycling schemes, energy-saving features and its own desalination plant, Los Fariones is fully entitled to call itself a 'biosphere hotel'. *248 rooms | Calle Acatife | tel. 928 51 01 75 | www.farioneshotels. com | Moderate–Expensive*

FARIONES PLAYA
The overbearing façade of dark lava rock is not to everyone's taste. But inside the beautifully designed gardens, which open towards the sea, are much admired. *231 rooms | Calle Acatife | tel. 928 51 34 00 | www.farioneshotels.com | Moderate*

INSIDER TIP ▶ FLORESTA
This spacious complex built in southern Spanish style consisting of 242 apartments is popular with families. Close to the beach. *Playa de los Pocillos | tel. 928 51 43 45 | www.hotel-floresta.de | Budget–Moderate*

JAMEOS PLAYA ★ ☺
This large and convivial hotel is both family-friendly and, because it operates energy-saving systems, environmentally friendly. This warm atmosphere is evident as soon as you enter the entrance lobby overlooked by wooden balconies in traditional Canarian style. The bright rooms are furnished with wooden furniture and the beach is on the doorstep. *530 rooms | Playa de los Pocillos | tel. 928 51 17 17 | www.seaside-hotels.de | Moderate–Expensive*

NAUTILUS
Quiet apartment complex approx. 15 minutes on foot from the beach. Occasional flight noise. *70 rooms | Calle Gramillo 5 | Urbanización Matagorda | tel. 928 51 44 00 | www.nautilus-lanzarote.com | Budget*

SAN ANTONIO
This traditional four-star is one of the few hotels that can rightly claim to be by the sea, namely the broad Playa de los Pocillos. Many of the rooms have a view over the sea toward Fuerteventura; large freshwater and seawater pool in the subtropical garden, plus glazed sauna with view of the heavens. Excellent buffets changing daily, shows in the evening, tennis courts, casual atmosphere. *331 rooms | Av. de las Playas 84 | tel. 928 51 42 00 | www.hotelsanantonio. com | Moderate–Expensive*

SOL LANZAROTE
Reputable hotel with one major plus point: direct access to the beach *348 rooms | Calle Grama 2 | tel. 928 51 48 88 | www.solmelia.com | Moderate*

INFORMATION

OFICINA MUNICIPAL DE TURISMO
Avda de las Playas, opposite the Centro Comercial La Geria | tel. 928 51 33 51 | www.ayuntamientodetias.es

WHERE TO GO

LA GERIA ★
The countryside around La Geria could be mistaken for the work of a bril-

liant landscape architect. The main route through the region runs from Mozaga (124 B3–4) (*ⓂE 8*) in the centre of the island via Masdache (127 F2) (*ⓂD 9*) as far as Uga in the south (127 D3) (*ⓂC 10*). The awesome vine region near the volcanic mountains appears to be even more intensively farmed when approached from the minor roads, such as from the road to La Vegueta (127 E3) (*ⓂD–E 8*). What is hard to believe is that nature itself initially brought new life to the barren land in the form of the delicate, grey-green lichen. Only much, much later did farmers move into vegetable and fruit growing, creating new plots of arable land.

The main bodegas are beside the main road, most of them opening from 10.30am to 6pm. The *El Grifo* winery *(LZ 30, km 11 | tel. 928 52 49 51 | www. elgrifo.com)* has a wine museum *(admission 4 euros)* where tools, some of which are over 200 years old, are exhibited. The *Bodegas Barreto (LZ 30, km 11 | tel. 928 52 07 17)* can offer a wide selection of wines from 7 to 9 euros (tasting included). The new bodega **INSIDER TIP** *Stratvs (LZ 30, km 18 | tel. 928 80 99 77 | www. stratvs.com)* is cool and ultra-modern. After only a few years on the market, their wines have won an incredible number of international awards. What is so striking about the winery, built unobtrusively into a shallow depression, is the architecture. Take the guided tour to see the vast, church-like presentation area with its line of towering wooden vats, then stroll along panoramic galleries into the heart of the winery. Sample a drop and judge the quality of the wines for yourself. Guided tours are held several times every day *(10 euros incl. tasting | phone in advance for an appointment)*. A bistro *(closed Mon | Moderate)* with a terrace serves freshly prepared snacks.

The atmospheric *El Aljibe del Obispo (Expensive)* opens at 7pm; as well as selling Stratvs wines the elegant gastro shop also sells award-winning cheeses bearing the Finca de Uga name.

The 🌿 *Bodega La Geria (LZ 30, km 19 | tel. 928 17 31 78 | www.lageria.com)* is situated directly opposite a fine dragon tree. If you make a tour through the *Bodegón Rubicón (LZ 30, km 19) | tel. 928 80 26 32 | www.vinosrubicon.com)*, a restored historic house, you will be shown the beautiful wine cellar and old presses before you get a chance to sample the wines. This rather primitive bodega is a little out of the way, accessible via a rough track. ● 🌿 *El Chupadero (LZ 30, km 18.8) | tel. 928 17 31 15 | www. el-chupadero.com | Moderate)* does not offer free tasting, but instead there's a friendly tapas bar with a terrace. Potential purchasers can sit on the terrace and unhurriedly snack on Mediterranean delicacies and sip the house wines. There is a view over thousands of mini-craters cradling the precious vines.

MANCHA BLANCA (123 D–E3) (*ⓂD 8*)

In 1735 streams of lava poured out of the Timanfaya volcanoes and advanced relentlessly on the little village. In desperation the inhabitants made one final attempt to avert the imminent catastrophe: they placed a statue of the village patron saint, Nuestra Señora de los Dolores, in front of the glowing lava as it edged ever closer. And it worked. The molten lava came to a standstill right in front of the figure. By way of thanks, the villagers built the church Iglesia de los Dolores on the edge of the village. It was after this eruption that the Virgen de los Dolores was proclaimed to be Señora de los Volcanes – Our Lady of the Volcanoes. She then became the island's patron saint. On the road to Timanfaya

National Park, you will pass the Visitor Centre (p. 75).

MOZAGA (124 B3–4) (*E 8*)

On the roundabout just outside this little village stands one of Manrique's largest pieces, the *Monumento al Campesino*, the Peasants' Monument. It was built at the end of the 1960s to draw attention to the worsening plight of the farmers. Appropriately it comprises water tanks from old fishing boats elevated on a platform of rocks. It serves as a blunt reminder that the island does not have an inexhaustible supply of resources.

Nearby is the ⭐ *Casa Museo del Campesino* (daily 10am–6pm / admission free), an arts and crafts museum housing domestic artefacts that reflect the life of the rural population. Visitors to the museum can watch craftsmen and women at work and purchase their products. As well as watching embroiderers and weavers (only occasionally) at work, the activities in pottery workshop are of special interest The artisans here make *novios de mojón:* originally, these clay figure couples with their exaggerated sexual organs were made by the early inhabitants as fertility symbols and exchanged between young couples. Traditionally the man would send a male figure to his girlfriend as way of a marriage proposal. If she accepted she would send a female version back to him.

The lower part of the old farmhouse houses a ● restaurant in lava vaults, serving typical Lanzarotean dishes. In the livelier bar on the ground floor you can sit on a gleaming white terrace, view the monumento and eat Lanzarotean tapas. Daily / tel. 928 52 01 36 / Moderate

The Béthencourt family run the **INSIDER TIP** *Caserío de Mozaga* in a grand 18th-century country house. This delightful hotel (8 rooms / Mozaga 8 / tel.

928 52 00 60 / www. caseriodemozaga. com / Moderate) also boasts a superb restaurant (daily 8pm–11pm / Expensive). The Finca Isabel (Calle Malva 11 / tel. 6 09 74 21 63 / www.fincaisabel.com / Budget–Moderate) situated amid fruit trees and vineyards has four apartments and a volcanic pool.

PLAYA QUEMADA (127 D4) (*C 11*)

A translation of quemada is 'burnt', a reference to the fact that the beach here is black and stony. There are a few houses (some of them holiday lets) and one or two Canarian restaurants, but apart from that, there's little here to detain you.

If you would like to linger and explore the craggy coastline, try the offerings at the *Restaurant Salmarina (Avda. Marítima 13 / tel. 928 17 35 62 / www.salmarina*

Monumento al Campesino: Manrique's homage to the peasants

Stopping-off point for transatlantic sailors: the beautiful marina at Puerto Calero

restaurante). Sit here right by the water in a part-maritime, part-rustic ambience and enjoy good quality fish and seafood without any frills.

PUERTO CALERO (127 E4) (𝄂 *D 10*)

The marina designed by the Lanzarotean architect Luís Ibáñez Margalef has already had to be extended. Many sailors stop off here on their way from Europe to America. Even if you are not an ocean-going mariner, it is worth a visit. Sailing trips including five-hour catamaran tours depart from here *(daily 11am–3.30pm | 59 euros | tel. 928 51 30 22 | www.cat lanza.com).* Another option is a descent to the sea-bed in a ● submarine *(Submarine Safaris: dives 10am, 11am, noon, 2pm | from 30 euros | tel. 928 51 28 89 | www.submarinesafaris.com).*

When this guide went to print, the *Museo de Cetáceos (Edif. Antiguo Varadero, 1ª planta, Local 11)* was closed for an indefinite period. Visitors to this sea-life museum gained insights into the world of whales and dolphins, with film clips and sound recordings, skeletons and models. The **INSIDER TIP** *Restaurant Amura (closed Mon | tel. 928 51 31 81 | Expensive)* was designed in the style of Southern-

state villa with a large veranda and palm terrace. Located at the end of the marina it serves imaginative fusion dishes. The Spanish king likes to dine here, when he is visiting Lanzarote.

The four-star Iberostar *Costa Calero (324 rooms | tel. 928 84 95 95 | www.ibero star.com | Expensive),* minimalist in style and finished in Mediterranean colours, is renowned for its great buffets and wide range of activities, including water sports and an all-day entertainment programme. The thermal indoor pool in the ● Roman-inspired spa extends deep into the garden. Other facilities include bike hire, diving equipment and thalassotherapy.

SAN BARTOLOMÉ (124 B4) (𝄂 *E 9*)

An unusual attraction in this otherwise sleepy town is the *Museo Etnográfico Tanit.* A beautifully renovated bodega in an 18th-century villa houses a museum displaying artefacts from rural life (tools, clothes, furniture, etc.) Other features include a wine cellar crammed full of barrels, a gallery with changing exhibitions and also a museum shop. *Mon–Sat 10am–2pm | Calle Constitución 1 | admission 6 euros | www.museotanit.com*

TIAGUA (123 F3) (*ω E 8*)

Tiagua, a neat and well-kept farming village, is worth a visit in its own right, but as it is also home to the ★ *Museo Agrícola El Patio,* it is definitely worth a detour. Shortly after it opened in 1994, the museum, which is housed in an old, but well-preserved farmhouse surrounded by a luxuriant garden, received the Canarian Culture prize. All the displays, from the bodega to the gofio mill, are in full working order.

The stables and working area are situated close to the windmill; unfortunately its sails were damaged badly by a tornado. Also in this section are the bodega (with wine tasting) and stables, where a herd of goats, a dromedary and a mule are kept. Old photographs and pottery that was used on the farm are displayed in the farmhouse. Also exhibited in the museum is a collection of beautiful lava stones and rocks. Adjoining the farmhouse are the old winery buildings with a collection of heavy presses and oak barrels. Wine tastings are held in the museum and you can buy bottles here. *Mon–Fri 10am–5.30pm, Sat 10am–2.30pm | admission 6 euros including a small sample of wine*

TINAJO, PLAYA DE TENEZA, PLAYA DE LA MADERA

Not spectacular, but very pretty, is the long and narrow village of *Tinajo* (124 B3) (*ω E 8*). A good place to eat here is *Mezzaluna (closed Mon | Avenida La Cañada 22 | tel. 928840141 | Budget–Moderate)*, where all the Italian classics are served – and that means pizzas from a charcoal oven. Some way from the centre of the village an unmarked road leads to the west coast and the ☽ *Playa de Teneza* (123 D2) (*ω C–D 7*), then on rough tracks to the *Playa de la Madera* on the edge of Timanfaya National Park

(122 C3) (*ω B 8*). The Atlantic waves often break powerfully on both beaches, with the seething waters making an impressive natural spectacle. If you swim here, stay in shallow waters. All too often bathers drown on the west coast, because they underestimate the immense suction power in the retreating sea and are dragged underwater. Now drive towards Caleta de Famara. En route it is worth making the climb to the old ☽ Playa de Teneza mill. Stop for a minute and admire the impressive view over the village and the Riscos de Famara mountain range.

A glimpse of how they used to live on the farm: Tiagua

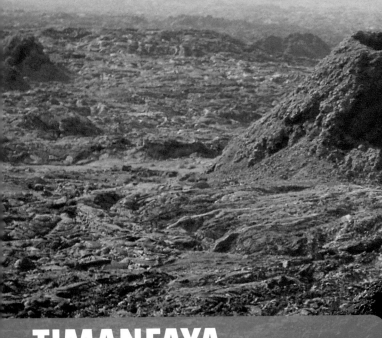

TIMANFAYA NATIONAL PARK

What a sight! The sea of black lava extends for miles. Towering above it in the distance are mountains, many with decapitated peaks. Others rise gently, but all are covered with granules of lava shimmering in a range of colours from beige and grey to rust-red.

Clouds cast bizarre shadows, the wind scurries across the plain, whistling between jagged chunks of magma, stirring up the tiny lapilli, the lava shingle that lies in layers three feet deep. These droplets of molten or semi-molten lava are known on the Canaries as picón. Not a single tree or shrub interrupts the monotony. It's a lunar landscape.

The *Montañas del Fuego*, the Fire Mountains, evoke a degree of trepidation in everyone who visits this desolate region. One of the worst catastrophes recorded in the history of the modern world happened here. The volcanic eruptions on Lanzarote lasted for six years, from 1730 to 1736. They buried almost a quarter of the island and left behind the largest field of lava in the world. The priest from Yaiza, Andrés Lorenzo Curbelo, began to write his diary on the night of 1 September 1730, the day the earth cracked open and started to spit fire. Almost every day he described the terrible events that were afflicting his island. Eventually, like many lanzaroteños, he fled to Gran Canaria. Many places were either buried by clouds of ash or devastated by streams of lava that flowed on into the sea. Millions of fish died, only to wash up

Photo: Volcanic landscape in Timanfaya National Park

The place that brought catastrophe to Lanzarote: an inferno still burns beneath the Montañas del Fuego

later along the coast. New mountains rose, craters were formed and exploded on the same day, chasms opened up. The heat burnt the fields and cattle succumbed to the poisonous vapours. In 1824 the peace was shattered again. Three more volcanoes were formed but the devastation bore no comparison to what had happened in the previous century.

Now everything has solidified. The immense power of the volcanic forces can be viewed and admired in safety.

The LZ 67 road from Yaiza to Mancha Blanca crosses the forbidding *malpaís*, the 'badlands' of solid magma. Rising on the left are the thirty or so cones of the Montañas del Fuego, among them the 1675-foot Timanfaya, surrounded by equally impressive companions. The colours gleam in the sun. The fluorescence is caused by the different minerals in the lava. This collection of conical hills are part of the Timanfaya National Park, a large part of which the road crosses. At the *dromedary station*, which you reach at the entrance to the Timanfaya National Park, more than a hundred of these beasts await the arrival of their next passengers. Do stop and take a break here. A ride on a ★ *dromedary* through the peace and stillness of the Timanfaya volcanic mountains is one of the most exciting things you can do on Lanzarote *(daily 9am–16pm | duration approx. 20 minutes | 12 euros per dromedary)*. Nearby is a bar, a shop selling souvenirs and a small museum exhibiting lava stones from the national park *(Mon–Fri 8am–3pm)*.

The journey continues. The following ⬃ pass affords a magnificent view over the sea of lava. Here the access road to the centre of the Timanfaya National Park forks off. The symbol for the park, a malevolent-looking demon, El Diablo, welcomes you to his kingdom. The devil idea is another product of César Manrique's fertile imagination.

TIMANFAYA NATIONAL PARK

(122–123 A–D 3–5) (⬥ B–C 8–9) **The national park was established in 1974. It is 20 square miles in area and its name is derived from a village that disappeared under the lava.**

From the LZ 67 a narrow asphalt road branches off to a cabin made from dark lava stone. After paying the admission fee continue for another two miles to the Islote de Hilario, a vantage point rising from the flat landscape like an islet (islote). At its summit are a visitor centre and the ⬃ *Restaurante del Diablo (Moderate)*, the 'Devil's Restaurant' that Manrique built from lava stone and fireproof materials. Panoramic windows with views in all directions surround the circular building. Even if you don't want to eat, look out the glass across the bleak, lava-strewn landscape. On a massive barbecue powered by heat from the centre of the earth, cooks grill steaks and fish, while outside park wardens demonstrate what is happening below the thin crust of lava. Brushwood is thrown into a shallow pit outside the restaurant and ignites spontaneously. When a bucket of water is emptied into a metre-deep hole, seconds later an explosive geyser of steam emerges. At a depth of 10 cm the temperature is 140º C/284º F, at 6 m it's 400º C/752 ºF. *Daily 9am–5.45pm, entry until 5pm | admission 8 euros*

SIGHTSEEING

RUTA DE LOS VOLCANES ★ ⬃
(122 C4) (⬥ B–C 9)
The highlight of the national park is the 45-minute journey along the six-mile vol-

cano route. It is not open to private cars; the only way to explore the park is a bus tour from the Islote de Hilario. The tour goes deep into a surreal world, where it seems as if dozens of meteorites have struck the earth, each forming its own craters. It's a lesson in vulcanology: look out for the steep-sided hornitos (small openings that release small quantities of lava to form stacks) or 100 m diameter calderas (craters formed by the collapse of land following an eruption). There are collapsed lava tunnels and huge ash slides. As the bus continues its journey through hell you listen to heroic music by Wagner and Beethoven, as if the landscape wasn't already dramatic enough, and the diary entries of the priest from Yaiza who witnessed the eruptions of 1730 that changed Lanzarote so drastically. *Departures every 30 minutes, last bus 5pm | bus tour included in the national park admission price*

The hot earth will set brushwood alight at the Islote de Hilario

CENTRO DE VISITANTES ●
(123 D3) (*ΩΩ D 8*)

The architecturally stunning Timanfaya National Park visitor centre explains the background to the Fire Mountains using interactive panels, exhibitions, photographs, a film and lava to touch. It also deals with the culture and the everyday life of the island's inhabitants. A boardwalk takes visitors a long way out onto the inhospitable expanse of black clinker. For a closer look at the volcanoes, another guided tour, the *Ruta de Tremesana* (126 C2) (*ΩΩ B–C 9*), follows a route along the southern edge of the national park for a more detailed lesson in volcanic geology. The path leads through a range of landscapes, including craters and lava tubes and an almost level lava lake. During the fascinating tour it becomes clear just how painstakingly, but ultimately successfully, nature has reclaimed this hostile wilderness. *Daily 9am–5pm | on the LZ 67, one mile from Mancha Blanca en route to the entrance to the park | tel. 928 84 08 39 | admission free | free walks usually Mon, Wed and Fri; two groups, each with eight participants, meet at 10am, book well in advance. (see Low Budget box)*

⭐ **Dromedary rides**
A ride through the volcanic ash fields in Timanfaya National Park on the back of a dromedary is an amazing experience → p. 74

⭐ **Ruta de los Volcanes**
The highlight of any visit to Timanfaya is a tour through the park's lunar landscape → p. 74

MARCO POLO HIGHLIGHTS

PLAYA BLANCA AND THE SOUTH

It's not unlike the Sahara Desert: barren land, parched by the sun, a few scrubby growths of lichen and dried grasses – the desert can have a mesmerising effect.

Although small thorn bushes cling tenaciously to the soil and spiky globes wave in the wind like a scene from a Western film, the pool, the beach and a cooling drink are never far away. Faintly visible in the heat, a settlement of white, low-rise buildings shimmers in the distance. Approach a little closer and it grows into a jumble of villas and hotels: Playa Blanca. The southern end of the island is by far the driest region of Lanzarote. The burnt and arid land, in which only a few wolfberry and euphorbia plants thrive, may initially deter exploration, but in the end many holidaymakers cannot resist taking a closer look. The sun always seems to shine in this part of the island. This is also why in the early 1980s the originally non-descript fishing village of Playa Blanca quickly became one of the island's three main tourist centres. Get away from the mega-resort and you will see some magnificent beaches, including the island's most popular nudist beaches. Opposite lies the island of Fuerteventura and a small offshore island, Isla de Lobos. Ferries shuttle across the water to the neighbouring islands and pleasure cruises explore the inshore waters.

Photo: Playas de Papagayo near Playa Blanca

The perfect destination for weather-distressed northern Europeans: sunshine and holiday fun are guaranteed in Lanzarote's hot south

PLAYA BLANCA

(126 B5–6) (Ⓜ A–B 11–12) **Once there was just a remote fishing village in this barren region, now there's a sprawling conurbation of whitewashed holiday villages.**

The architecture of the villas and hotels is worth a closer look, and luxuriant gardens awash with colourful bougainvillea do wonders for the overall impression of Playa Blanca (pop. 10,000). This resort is perfect for families and mature couples. Its plus points are proximity to the fantastic Playas de Papagayo and the almost unbroken sunshine.

The spacious, pedestrianised promenade is the focal point for holidaymakers. At the town beach the atmosphere is family-oriented, and the restaurants and apartments are restricted to a height of two or three storeys. Heading westwards, the promenade continues for miles to the lighthouse, *Faro de Pechiguera*. To the east, it extends from the ferry port ontory for fine views along the colourful cliffs as far as the nearby Papagayo beaches, over the Marina Rubicón and, if the weather is fine, to Fuerteventura.

There are countless restaurants on Playa Blanca's promenade

as far as the vast *Marina Rubicón* and the *Castillo de las Coloradas*. Unfortunately the largest hotels are clustered on the finest beaches. Row after row of villa and apartment complexes have slowly crept inland onto the parched plain.

SIGHTSEEING

CASTILLO DE LAS COLORADAS ☆

Even down here on the south coast, the fishing communities were not immune from pirate attacks, and the villages were repeatedly pillaged. It is said that the island's conqueror, Jean de Béthencourt, once built a fortress here. The present castle dates from 1789. Its name derives from the colourful *(coloradas)* rocks along this section of the coast. Unfortunately the massive circular tower is not open to visitors and is now partially blocked off by hotels. It is worth making the trip to the Punta del Águila prom-

FOOD & DRINK

EL ALMACÉN DE LA SAL

Here, in one of the town's oldest buildings, salt collected from the Salinas de Janubio was stored. In 1994, the house was restored at great expense and has been converted into a high-class restaurant. It's worth taking a peep inside. However, the chef's achievements fall short of the stylish ambience. If all you want is a coffee or a cool drink on the terrace, then you can't go wrong. *Closed Tue | on the promenade near the main roundabout | tel. 928 51 78 85 | www.almacendelasal.com | Expensive*

AROMAS YAIZA

Creative Canarian cuisine served in an alley behind the main shopping street. A regular haunt of well-heeled locals, mainly on account of the fresh fish *a la espalda*, ('pan-fried on its back') or the tender sucking pig. And the Lanzarote wine flows freely too! *Closed Sun | Calle La Laja 1 | tel. 928 34 96 91 | Moderate*

INSIDER TIP ▸ BAR ONE ●

Whatever the time of day, this is the perfect place to chill out over a snack, while watching the yachts come and go. Inexpensive lunch-time menu. *Daily | Marina Rubicón | tel. 928 34 99 30 | Budget–Moderate*

BODEGÓN LAS TAPAS

Tapas consumed in large quantities in this rustic setting surrounded by wine barrels. Overlooking the promenade and the sea. *Closed Sun | Paseo Marítimo 5 | tel. 928 51 83 10 | Moderate*

CAFÉ DEL MAR ●

Like its counterpart, the Café del Mar in Ibiza, it's popular for its chill-out music, stylish pastel decor, relaxed atmosphere and cheerful staff. Great location by the marina. Renowned for mega-parties at full moon. *Daily | Marina Rubicón | tel. 928 34 92 00 | www.cafedelmarmusic.com | Budget*

CASA PEDRO

Fish to die for. It simply melts on the tongue. If you're feeling hungry, then start with the house speciality, homemade fish soup. *Daily | Avda. Marítima 17 | tel. 928 51 79 65 | Moderate*

LA CASA ROJA

The 'red house' with its panoramic windows sits on a wooden pier overlooking the marina crammed with smart yachts. Setting elegant, cuisine upmarket Mediterranean with the emphasis on fish and seafood. *Daily | Marina Rubicón | tel. 928 51 96 44 | Moderate*

LA COFRADÍA

Canteen-style ambience and view of a boatyard. People come here purely for the fresh fish, prepared in the 'fisherman's guild' *(cofradía)* to simple but delicious recipes. But it is not cheap. *Daily | opposite the ferry terminal | tel. 928 34 90 66 | Moderate*

SHOPPING

Take care if shopping for photographic equipment. The shops in the town centre are renowned for poor quality goods at rip-off prices.

★ **Femés**
The clear view from the balcón is spectacular → **p. 83**

★ **El Golfo**
The lagoon with its bottle-green colouring looks like something from another world → **p. 83**

★ **Los Hervideros**
The waves pound their way through rocky channels amid mountains of spray → **p. 84**

★ **Playas de Papagayo**
Golden yellow jewels: Lanzarote's finest beaches → **p. 85**

★ **Salinas de Janubio**
The Canary Islands' largest salt pans gleam in a multi-coloured array → **p. 85**

★ **Yaiza**
Model village with traditional white houses and green shutters → **p. 86**

MARCO POLO HIGHLIGHTS

FUNDACIÓN CÉSAR MANRIQUE

More from the grand master, even here in Playa Blanca. *Avda Papagayo 8*

MERCADILLO

Not unlike the Sunday market in Teguise, but smaller. *Wed and Sat 9am–2pm | Costa Papagayo and Marina Rubicón*

MYSTIC

Pamper yourself, but with natural materials: sponges, brushes and beach towels, plus a selection of esoteric music CDs. *Avda. Marítima s/n*

INSIDER TIP ROMY B

Light fabrics are the stuff of modern fashion – at least on Lanzarote. Locally-based designers, such as Romy B, design casual collections and accessories in high-quality linen. *Calle Limones 67 | www.romyb.info*

BEACHES

There are three fine bathing beaches in the resort itself: there's the lovely, sandy beach beneath the promenade near the town centre; to the west, beneath the Lanzarote Park hotel, the *Playa Flamingo* and finally east of the town beach the *Playa Dorada*. The last-named beaches have fine, golden sand and also loungers and parasols for hire. Breakwaters ensure totally safe bathing in clear water.

LEISURE & SPORTS

Apart from swimming and diving, you can also hire a pedalo *(on the Playa Dorada, 6 euros per person)* or have fun in a speedboat or a banana boat *(in the harbour at Playa Blanca)*. Excursions in local waters leave from here. A number of boat operators run trips to the Papagayo beaches and the ● Isla de Lobos. A free bus takes guests to Puerto Calero for expeditions in a ● submarine *(from 30 euros | www.submarinesafaris.com)*.

All four- and five-star hotels in Playa Blanca have modern spa facilities. The town's no. 1 hotel is the *Hotel Princesa Yaiza,* where the health and beauty team use ingredients sourced on the island. The emphasis is on treatments that follow the correct medical and cosmetic guidelines. All therapists are professionally trained and multi-lingual *(Avda Papagayo 22 | www.princesayaiza.com)*.

ENTERTAINMENT

It's fun to sit and drink a glass of wine or a beer on the promenade and follow it with a cocktail in the Café del Mar in the marina. The *Jazz Club Cuatro Lunas* is held in the Hotel Princesa Yaiza every Thursday and Saturday evening. Expect to hear live music played by top-class bands. It's a bit livelier in the nearby *Centro Comercial Papagayo* in *Jungle's Bar disco club (daily 10pm–5am)*, for example, where it stays loud and animated until dawn. On the other side of the town centre, towards the Faro de Pechiguera,

LOW BUDGET

▶ *Los Hervideros*, a family-run restaurant, is the cheapest in Playa Blanca; ideal for low-budget lunch-time menus. *Closed Tue | Calle El Marisco 9 | tel. 928 51 77 07*

▶ The *Apartamentos Gutierrez* must be the cheapest place to spend the night in the centre of Playa Blanca (from 40 euros/double room) and near the beach too. *Plaza Nuestra Señora del Carmen 8 | Mobile 6 36 37 28 93*

Fancy a boat trip? Fishing and ferry harbour in Playa Blanca

the *Marea (daily 10pm–3.30am)* in the *Centro Comercial La Mulata* plays a mix of top forty, pop and funk.

WHERE TO STAY

GRAN CASTILLO ☙

This complex built in typical Andalusian style around a Spanish fantasy castle is situated by the sea near the Papagayo beaches. Spacious, attractive rooms, large pool area, view of Fuertaventura. *279 rooms | Urbanización Las Coloradas | tel. 928 59 59 99 | www.dreamplacehotels. com | Expensive*

GRAN MELIÁ VOLCÁN

A five-star hotel right beside the marina, to the east of Playa Blanca. The rooms are distributed around small two- and three-storey blocks, clustered together in the style of a Canarian village. *217 rooms | Urbanización Castillo del Aquila |*

tel. 928 51 91 85 | www.solmelia.com | Moderate

IBEROSTAR LANZAROTE PARK ☙

The hotel is perched on a cape jutting into the sea, only a few steps from the Flamingo beach. Studios painted in maritime colours with kitchenette and sea view balcony; rooms on the ground floor with direct access to the pool gardens are ideal for families. Good buffets, the 'dine around' idea is innovative, i.e. if you book half-board you can eat in the sister Papagayo Hotel. *Urbanización Montaña Roja | tel. 928 51 70 48 | www. iberostar.com | Moderate*

PARADISE ISLAND

With a varied layout on different levels, this apartment hotel scores with its garden, pools, bridges and waterfalls The complex is a mile from the beach. *278 rooms | Urbanización Montaña Roja | tel.*

928 51 78 80 | www.hotel-paradiseisland. com | Moderate

INSIDER TIP PRINCESA YAIZA ☆

The finest hotel in town: only the promenade separates this five-star hotel from the Playa Dorada. The architecture is Moorish, the interior colonial style, the atmosphere opulent. All the rooms are more like suites; they have a kitchenette and dressing room, and have a view over to Fuerteventura. One major plus point is the restaurant food, which includes constantly changing, haute cuisine buffets. Another impressive feature is *Kikoland*, a 10,000-square-metre children's area with mini-pool and adventure playground. In addition: pools and spa, squash and tennis courts. 385 rooms | *Avda Papagayo | tel. 928 51 92 22 | www. princesayaiza.com | Expensive*

TIMANFAYA PALACE

A four-star hotel with Moorish architectural features, still comfortable, but perhaps its glitzier days are in the past. Still, its location on the promenade is first-class and the Playa Flamingo only ten minutes away on foot. *305 rooms | Urbanización Montaña Roja | tel. 928 51 76 76 | www.h10hotels.com | Expensive*

INFORMATION

OFICINA DE TURISMO

Calle Limones / Avda de Papagayo | tel. 928 51 81 50 | www.ayuntamientodeyaiza. es; there's another information pavilion by the yachting marina: *Kiosco Marina.*

Science fiction supernatural with a natural cause: algae colour the El Golfo lagoon green

WHERE TO GO

FARO DE PECHIGUERA ☀
(126 A6) (*M A 12*)

There is a good road to the lighthouse, which lies two miles west of the town, but the pleasant walk to this conspicuous landmark only takes about an hour. The path follows the coastline, passing the new hotels and apartment complexes on the shoreline. Built in 1986 under the aegis of the ubiquitous Cesar Manrique, the lighthouse is not in itself particularly impressive, but the views over to the islands of Los Lobos and Fuerteventura are wonderful.

FEMÉS ★ ☀ (126 C4) (*M B 10*)

The name, Balcón de Femés, is fully justified. If the weather is fine, from this

pass at 1475 ft you get an amazing view over the Rubicón plain, far beyond Playa Blanca and across to Isla de Lobos and Fuerteventura. Femés is not much more than a cluster of houses, but the village can boast three decent restaurants. Eat in the ☀ *Balcón de Femés (daily | tel. 928 83 63 51 | Moderate)* and you are sitting right on the viewing platform. The *Casa Emiliano (closed Mon | tel. 928 83 02 23 | Moderate),* on the other hand, is a set back a little, but has superb food and a pretty terrace. The *Restaurante Femés (daily | Budget)* is on the plaza. There is no view, but the locals eat here. Try the goat's cheese from Femés.

FUERTEVENTURA (0) (*M A 14*)

It only takes 35 minutes for the ferry to cross from Playa Blanca to the harbour at Corralejo on the larger neighbouring island. It leaves on the hour from 7am and the last return crossing is scheduled for 8pm (return journey for 1 person 32–40 euros) *See Trips & tours (p. 91) for a detailed description of day trip to Fuerteventura.*

EL GOLFO ★ ☀ (126 B2) (*M A 9*)

Like the Fire Mountains, the deep green El Golfo lagoon has also featured in many a science-fiction movie. Shaped like a sickle, the lake fills a sunken volcanic crater, half of which is in a cove by the sea. The walls of the crater have been eroded by wind. What makes this lake such an attraction is the unusual colour of the water. Sea water, which after evaporation has a higher salt content, remains trapped in the crater and, due to special algae, then turns a bright green. The contrast with the tar-black lava sand, the dark blue Atlantic and the white spray is striking. Access: from the car-park by the country lane to the south of the lagoon and from the car-park on the

The seething Atlantic:
Los Hervideros

left at the edge of the village of El Golfo. The country lane ends on the other side of the lagoon in the fishing village of El Golfo. It's perhaps hard to believe, but the entire village, together with hotel

and restaurants, is threatened with demolition. According to Spanish law, houses less than 100 m from the sea at low tide are illegal. As houses in similar coastal locations elsewhere in the Canaries have been summarily torn down, the inhabitants of El Golfo fear the worst.

Despite the threat hanging over the village, it can still boast some of the best fish restaurants in Lanzarote. If the weather is poor and the boats can't make it out to their fishing grounds, the restaurants have no choice but to close because they run out of supplies. Could there be a better guarantee of freshness? The best restaurants: *Lago Verde (closed Tue | Avda Marítima 46 | tel. 928 17 33 11)*, *Mar Azul (daily | Avda Marítima 42 | tel. 928 17 31 32)* and **INSIDER TIP** Bogavante for its spectacular location right at the sea edge *(daily | Avda Marítima 39 | tel. 928 17 35 05 | all Expensive*

El Hotelito is lovely place to stay. This 'miniature hotel' has only nine rooms, some with a sea view. The proprietor, Isabel, will ensure you get personal service. This hotel is a refuge for independent travellers looking for total peace and tranquillity. *Tel. 928 17 32 72 | Budget*

LOS HERVIDEROS ⭐
(126 B3) (*🛱 A 10*)

The water bubbles and hisses at Los Hervideros (literally 'the boiling waters'), which lie between the Salinas de Janubio and El Golfo. But in fact it's got nothing to do with heat. This impressive spectacle of caves, chimneys and arches has occurred through tidal erosion of the porous lava rock. At high tide, and especially when the Atlantic is rough and heavy swells roll in, the water crashes up into the air with great force. A set of angled paths and staircases lead to a viewing platform. A surfaced car-park is located at the side.

INSIDER TIP ▶ MONTAÑA ROJA ☼
(126 A–B 5–6) (*Ⓜ A 11*)

If visitors to Playa Blanca need some exercise after too much lounging around on the beach, it's not far to Montaña Roja. It is an easy climb to the top of the Red Mountain (636 ft), the nearest volcano to Playa Blanca, and the only elevation on the southern El Rubicón plain. The ascent starts above the Montaña Baja holiday complex along a well-worn, easily visible footpath and it takes not much longer than half an hour. At the top there is an equally good footpath around the entire crater. The view from up here encompasses Playa Blanca and the Papagayo beaches to the east, while to the south Fuerteventura is usually clearly visible. Further west, endless apartment blocks, some only half-finished, spoil the panoramic view.

PLAYAS DE PAPAGAYO ⭐
(126 C6) (*Ⓜ B 12*)

The beaches some 2 to 3.5 miles east of Playa Blanca are renowned for their beauty. Framed by rocks, the beaches here are covered with fine, golden sand, they are not desecrated by tar or rubbish and the turquoise water is beautifully clean. In addition, the currents are usually weak and the waves gentle, so that children can safely swim and paddle. The beaches are only accessible by car via a signposted track (3 euros). The admission charge also includes entry to the nature reserve, the *Monumento Natural de los Ajaches*, which lies behind the beaches. Large car-parks are to be found near the Playa Mujeres, above the Playa Papagayo and by the wilder Playa Caleta del Congrio. The Papagayo beaches can easily be reached INSIDER TIP ▶ in only 15 minutes on foot from the district of Las Coloradas. ● Park on the road in front of the Papagayo Arena Hotel and follow the signposted footpath to the south. This way you avoid the rough track and save 3 euros.

All beaches are easy to access, even the highly recommended smaller ones: Playa del Pozo, Playa de la Cera and Playa de Puerto Muelas. When the tide is out, you can walk from one beach to the next.

SALINAS DE JANUBIO ⭐ ●
(126 B4) (*Ⓜ A–B 10*)

Forming long rows of rectangular fields in varying sizes in iridescent browns, reds, greys and blacks and resembling a giant patchwork quilt, the Saline de Janubio is situated below the road to Playa Blanca. Sea salt used to be of vital importance for the fishing community, as it was needed

BORN IN HELL

You often find them on the black lava beaches on the west coast: small, green, shimmering pebbles of ● olivine. The mineral was hurled upwards from the bowels of the earth together with the magma and later washed out of the clinker by the sea. Pieces of lava studded with olivine are sold as souvenirs, e.g. at Los Hervideros and El Golfo, for 1 to 3 euros. Many other shops sell jewellery using this pretty semi-precious stone. However, most of it comes not from the island but from South America and Asia, as the fragments found on Lanzarote are usually too small.

to conserve the precious catch. Wind pumps, which have fallen into disrepair, pumped the seawater up 40 m into the largest pond. From there it was gradually discharged into the smallest pond, but only after undergoing a series of ingenious evaporation stages. The workers then collected the crystallised salt into mounds using special wooden rakes.

During the 19th century, the salt pans extracted more than 10,000 tons of salt every year. It is no longer commercially viable to work the salt pans on a large scale. Only small quantities are harvested now. To get a closer look at the whole complex, approach the salt pans from the attractive beach below.

Above it is the ☆ *Mirador Salinas restaurant.* Sit on its glassed-in terrace and admire the extensive view over the salt pans. The colours are beautiful at sunset. It is also possible to buy the ⏱ coarse-grained and tasty sea salt here. It is rich in calcium, magnesium and iodine. The top layer of salt, known as flor de sal (literally 'flower of salt') is especially rich in minerals. *Closed Thu | tel. 928 17 30 70 | Moderate*

UGA (127 D3) (*∅ C 10*)

This tiny, oasis-like village with dazzling white, cuboid houses, palm trees and an African-sounding name is also home to the dromedaries, which trek across the Fire Mountains bearing day-trippers. When their day's work is done, they are usually to be seen passing the Uga–Yaiza roundabout between 4.30pm and 5pm. Uga is also well known for its salmon smokehouse situated on the road to Arrecife. *Casa Gregorio* in the village *(closed Tue | tel. 928 83 01 08 | Budget–Moderate)* is highly regarded for its inexpensive and delicious Lanzarotean fare.

YAIZA ★ (126–127 C–D3) (*∅ B–C 10*)

This is what César Manrique wanted to see throughout the island: gleaming white houses, bright green window shutters and flowering geraniums. Yaiza is Lanzarote's model village and has already won several 'beauty competitions'. One particularly harmonious ensemble is to be found around the 17th-century church of Nuestra Señora de los Remedios and the two adjoining squares. It

CLUB LA SANTA

Sport and fitness are permanently on the agenda in the almost 30-year-old training centre on the north coast. Many different leisure pursuits from aerobics to triathlon are available to guests, and only to guests at the best-known sports club on the Canary Islands. The club has its own athletics stadium, a windsurfing lagoon, racing cycles and more. And then there are themed weeks on the martial arts or dancing and other events, such as tennis tournaments or courses on the subject of 'How do I change a cycle tyre'. Dozens of personal trainers are on hand to meet every whim. Supplements are only payable for golf and diving. Only the diving school can be booked from outside the club. Information and reservations: *Club La Santa: Club La Santa | 91 Walkden Road, Manchester M28 7BQ | tel. 061 790 9890 | www.clublasanta. com; La Santa Diving: tel. 928 59 99 95 | www.lasantadiving.com | basic course 75 euros, open water diver 475 euros*

Rustic-style conviviality in warm colours: the Finca de las Salinas

is worth taking a look inside the church with its exposed bells in the bell tower: the Madonna statue on the high altar is bathed in a mysterious blue light shining in through the church windows. Every year on 8 September, the figure leads a procession through the village.

Opposite the church is the low white *Casa de la Cultura (Mon–Fri 9am–1pm and 5pm–7pm)*, Yaiza's cultural centre. Built in the 19th century, it was from 1871 to 1937 the residence of the Spanish politician and writer, Benito Pérez Armas, and is now used for temporary exhibitions.

Artworks are also displayed in the INSIDERTIP *Galería Yaiza*. It houses pieces by Lanzarotean masters, such as César Manrique and Ildefonso Aguilar, Veno and Tayó *(Mon–Sat 5–7pm / Carretera General 13 / LZ-2)*. The former school, the *Antigua Escuela (La Cuesta 1 / LZ 2)*, at the opposite end of the village is also worth seeking out. Instead of classrooms, it houses a bistro-café and interesting shops selling jewellery and handicrafts. The range of goods in *La Route des Caravanes* is a scene from the Arabian Nights. An evocative place to spend the night is the INSIDERTIP *Finca de las Salinas (19 rooms / Calle La Cuesta 17 / tel. 928 83 03 25 / www.fincasalinas. com / Moderate–Expensive)*, an upmarket, rustic-style country hotel in an 18th-century building. The architecture is interesting and the renovation work attributable to the Lanzarotean architect Angel García Puertas. Fastidious service, attention to detail and a colourful atmosphere are just some of the attributes of its *Mariateresa* restaurant and the Bodega *Don Gonzalo (daily / Expensive)*. Another good choice is the ● *Casa de Hilario (7 rooms / Carretera García Escámez 19 / tel. 928 83 62 62 / www.casadehilario. com/ Expensive)*. The view from the pool terrace takes in the sea and the forbidding outline of the Fire Mountains. The rooms and lounges, eccentrically decorated with chinoiserie, hark back to a bygone age. See out the evening by the fireplace over a glass of wine.

TRIPS & TOURS

The tours are marked in green in the road atlas,
pull-out map and on the back cover

① THE SOUTH: OUT AND ABOUT IN VOLCANO LAND

Set out from Arrecife for the Monumento al Campesino and carry on to Tiagua, where you will enjoy the Museo Agricola El Patio, one of the island's most interesting museums. The tour continues to the strange volcanic wilderness of the Timanfaya National Park. Next comes the lagoon at El Golfo, via the model village of Yaiza. Now follow the coast road along the black lava coastline down to the salt pans at Janubio. The return journey takes in the vantage point at Femés, followed by La Geria. Return to Arrecife via Mozaga. This journey covers 53 miles.

Leave Arrecife on the LZ 20 to San Bartolomé , then on to the roundabout near Mozaga. The **Monumento al Campesino** is visible from here → p. 69. Next is **Tiagua** → p. 71 with its windmills and excellent open-air museum, the **Museo Agrícola El Patio**. The next place, **Mancha Blanca** → p. 68, is almost on the edge of Timanfaya National Park.

The **Centro de Visitantes** is situated on the right close to the lava fields → p. 75. The boundary of the **national park** → p. 74 is marked by wooden panels topped by the park's little devil symbol, the *Diablo de Timanfaya*. Turn right onto the narrow asphalt road that leads to the **Islote de Hilario**. A sightseeing bus runs from here via the **Ruta de los Volcanes** → p. 74 to some of the most

Photo: Yaiza

By car and on foot through Lanzarote's volcanic heartland – and a short detour to its larger neighbour: Fuerteventura

interesting places in the Fire Mountains. When you leave the national park and head towards Yaiza, you will come to the **dromedary station** → p. 74.

Yaiza → p. 86, a pretty town, gleaming brightly in green and white, contrasts starkly with the surrounding bleak landscape. It is regarded as a showpiece of Lanzarotean architecture. From the roundabout on the bypass to the west of Yaiza, the LZ 704 branches off to **El Golfo** → p. 83, the famous green lagoon on the west coast. The village of El Golfo is

known for its excellent fish restaurants. The LZ 703 coast road runs down from El Golfo to the next attraction: **Los Hervideros** → p. 84. A little further south is Lanzarote's largest salt extraction complex, the **Salinas de Janubio** → p. 85. Two decades ago, these rectangular evaporation ponds, laid out in a strict geometric pattern, were bustling with activity. Now production levels are a fraction of what they used to be. A road via **Playa Blanca** → p. 77 leads up to the ☀️ village of **Femés** → p. 83 for a spectacular view.

Follow the road from Femés through the upland valley and on to the Yaiza–Arrecife main road. Keep left here and on the outskirts of the African-looking village of **Uga** → p. 86, turn right on to the LZ 30 towards Masdache and La Geria. Beyond Uga you will see the famous **La Geria** wine-producing region → p. 67. Passing through what must be island's strangest landscape, the road goes through Masdache and continues to Mozaga, where you encounter Manrique's white Peasant's Monument again.

2 WALKS IN A SEA OF LAVA

Walking independently in the Timanfaya National Park is not allowed. But there are two routes which you can undertake independently. The first one follows the coast of the Fire Mountains, the second rises to an impressive 'white crater'. Robust footwear and plenty of drinking water are required for both tours.

The coastal path goes through inhospitable terrain, where there is nothing much to see apart from wild and unspoilt countryside. When it came into sudden contact with the cold water, the black lava often rose up and formed weird shapes. Travel from **Tinajo** → p. 71 by car initially on asphalt (2 mi) above the Playa de Teneza and later on wide sheets of corrugated iron (4 mi) as far as the black **Playa de la Madera** → p. 71. Start walking along the coast from here on what is for the most part a clearly identifiable path as far as the **Playa del Cochino**. Return to the starting point on the same footpath (there and back 4–5 hrs).

If you are exploring with friends, you can share cars and do the full, five-hour route from Playa de la Madera as far as the fishing village of **El Golfo** → p. 83. There are two advantages to this option: firstly you don't have to cover the same stretch twice, secondly you can finish off the day out with a delicious and richly-deserved fish supper. This is how you do it: Friends take you to the starting point

Wine production Lanzarotean-style: among the vines near La Geria

and collect you at the agreed time in El Golfo. Swap roles the following day. Alternatively, park the first of two vehicles at the end of the walk, then drive to the starting point in the second car.

One great walk, the highlight of which is a fantastic view, is the route to the **Caldera Blanca** (122–123 C–D3) *(∭ C 8)*. This a there-and-back walk which you can carry out under your own steam. The path is well marked, the ascent steep and strenuous in places. Be aware of one thing: you are making a challenging, four-hour walk on your own, so take plenty to drink and be sure that you and your companions are in good shape.

Leave the Timanfaya National Park on the LZ 67 and head towards Mancha Blanca. Just before you reach the village, a narrow tarred strip branches off to the left towards *Tinajo → p. 71*. At this point double back to the left onto a lava track and follow it for about 700 m. At the end, easily identified by three large chunks of lava, park the car. The rest of the walk is visible ahead, diagonally to the right. The route is marked by a red arrow and a pile of stone. Follow a stream of black lava for about 40 minutes. After completing about two thirds of this section, on the right is a hard-to-see but fine cave with long lava stalactites. The visual landmark for the first section is the red volcano cone.

At its foot and along a wall, continue for just under 10 minutes to the right and then again through a lava field (approx. 10 minutes), keeping the white cone, the Caldera Blanca, constantly in your sight. At the foot of the mountain, climb first up to the left, keeping constantly to the boundary between the white rock and the dark lava (approx. 10 minutes). Now continue climbing to the right up the volcano again for just under 10 minutes, always along the already identified chan-

nel. Contrary to expectations, the ground underfoot on the Fire Mountain is firm, light rock covered with grey-white lichen. Take particular care on the edge of the crater, as it is easy to go wrong. The ascent, which is an even climb via the left-hand semi-circle, takes at least 40 minutes and rises another 650 ft. When you finally arrive at the top, if it is a clear day, the view is stunning.

The descent is clockwise down the steeper side of the crater, before you take the same path in the opposite direction back to the starting point.

3 VISIT TO THE NEIGHBOURS: BY FERRY TO FUERTEVENTURA

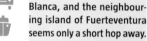

Look out to sea from Playa Blanca, and the neighbouring island of Fuerteventura seems only a short hop away. And it isn't far. The ferry to Corralejo takes barely half an hour. Even though most of the island consists of rock, it has some of the most impressive beaches in Europe. Like Lanzarote, it has a history of volcanic activity and its strange contours reflect that, but the last event was 7000 years ago. This journey covers 135 miles.

Ideally catch an early morning ferry, so that you have the whole day to get to know 'Fuerte'. *Fred Olsen Express (daily 8.30am, 10am, 2pm, 4pm, 6pm, Mon–Fri also 7.10am, return 9am, 11am, 3pm, 5pm, 7pm, Mon–Fri also 7.45am | return journey 50 euros per person, 4 persons with car 240 euros | Muelle Playa Blanca | tel. 902 10 01 07 | www.fredolsen.es)* and *Armas (daily 7am, 9am, 11am, 3pm, 5pm, 7pm, Fri/Sat also 1pm; return 8am, 10am, 2pm, 4pm, 6pm, 8pm, Fri/Sat also noon | 35 euros per person | Muelle Playa Blanca | tel. 902 45 65 00 | www.naviera armas.com)* operate a regular car and passenger service from Playa Blanca → p. 77 to Corralejo on Fuerteventura.

It is not usually worth taking a hire car on the ferry, as travellers who do not live permanently on Lanzarote are not entitled to the special tariff *(paquete de ahorro)* and in any case taking a hire car across the water is often not permitted for insurance reasons. Once you arrive on Fuerteventura you will see car rental firms, so you can make a quick tour of the island. The service offered by car rental company *Cabrera Medina/Cicar*, which has a branch in the harbour at Corralejo, is convenient *(reservations may also be made in one of the many offices on Lanzarote | tel. 928 82 29 00 | www.cicar.com).*

As you enter the harbour at Corralejo, you will see shimmering dunes and attractive coastal promenades, but save a stroll through the town until you return in the evening, while you are waiting for your return crossing to Lanzarote.

Leave Corralejo on the FV-101 towards the south through an arid, sun-baked landscape. Make your first stop in Villaverde, where you can explore a volcanic tube very similar to those on Lanzarote *(Cueva del Llano: Tue–Sun 10am–6pm, half-hour guided tours in English | admission 5 euros).* Return to the car and continue to La Oliva, the main town for the municipality of the same name. It's worth stopping to admire a number of fine 18th-century buildings, notably the Church of Nuestra Señora de Candelaria and the former 'house of the colonels' or Casa de los Coroneles *(Tue–Sun 10am–6pm, when exhibitions are in situ | Calle Juan Cabrera Méndez s/n | admission free)* with an art gallery surrounding a palm tree courtyard.

Now continue southwards through a desert landscape of striking volcanic cones. Pass Tindaya, the sacred mountain of

the aboriginal inhabitants, before reaching Tefía, where there is an interesting open-air museum, the Ecomuseo de la Alcogida *(Tue–Sat 10am–6pm | admission 5 euros).* Exhibits include restored farmhouses, mills and grain stores. A second open-air museum, the splendidly restored mill, Molino de Antigua *(Tue–Sat 10am–6pm | Ctra. FV-20 | admission 2 euros),* is on the outskirts of Antigua. Once beyond Tindaya, the landscape becomes much more mountainous. The road winds its way over bare hill-tops up to the Morro Veloso vantage point. Pass two enormous figures, portrayals of the last early Canarian rulers, and then turn left. Before long, you will find yourself outside a kind of farmhouse with a fantastic panoramic terrace (admission free). If visibility is good, the view extends as far as Lanzarote, Gran Canaria and Tenerife.

A series of hairpin bends leads down to the island's former capital, Betancuria. Despite a cathedral resembling a fortress, some splendid townhouses and the ruins of a monastery testifying to the settlement's more illustrious past, it now has the charm of a sleepy village The main place of interest is the Casa Santa María *(Mon–Sat 11am–3.30pm | admission 5 euros),* a superbly restored house with craft workshops, a garden café and restaurant; a multi-media screen showcases the island's best features.

After Betancuria you pass Vega de Río Palmas, an oasis of palm trees with a pilgrimage church. The landscape now starts to get more interesting. Ahead as far as the eye can see are reddish mountainous humps furrowed with gullies created by erosion, in between lonely valleys where few, if any, plants survive for long.

If you have time, make a detour from Pájara to the coastal village of Ajuy (altogether another 13 mi), where weathered white limestone cliffs contrast with the black lava beach.

Otherwise carry on through a seemingly endless sequence of valleys and peaks to **La Pared**, where you can cross the narrow, sandblown isthmus to Fuerteventura's east coast. Facing south are the resorts of **Costa Calma** and **Jandía**, both with magnificent beaches, but unless you've skipped some earlier stops, you will now have to head north to catch the last ferry back to Lanzarote. Possible stops when homeward bound include the animal park and botanical gardens at **Oasis Park** *(daily 9am–6pm | Ctra. FV-2, km 57.6 | admission 18 euros | www. fuerteventuraoasispark.com)* in **La Lajita**, the salt flats at **Salinas del Carmen**

(Museo de la Sal: Tue–Sat 10am–6pm | admission 5 euros) and **Puerto del Rosario**. It's worth pausing in the island's capital for a stroll along the promenade above a few small beaches and passing restaurants with terraces and maritime sculptures against a backdrop of large cruise ships.

Finally take the FV-1 (when not closed for nature conservation reasons) across a vast landscape of dunes to Corralejo: a crystal-clear, turquoise sea and miles of white sand blown into sickle-shaped arcs by the wind. This will be your last chance for a dip in the sea, but you may prefer to wander through the atmospheric old town of Corralejo, before catching the ferry back to Lanzarote.

Do we really have to go back to Lanzarote? The idyllic beach at Jandía on Fuerteventura

SPORTS & ACTIVITIES

Because a constant wind is pretty well guaranteed, windsurfing is the number one water activity on Lanzarote. But given the good thermal currents, paragliding and hang gliding have also gained in popularity.

Lanzarote is also a great destination for cyclists and hikers. The guided walks in the Timanfaya National Park explore some extraordinary landscapes and leave a lasting impression *(see Trips & Tours)*. Diving schools run courses and organise dives at interesting locations and then there's golf, riding, fishing and deep-sea fishing. If that is not enough, many holiday centres have tennis and squash courts. Other special events include (usually only from May to December) beach volleyball tournaments,

cycle races and marathon running. One competition that attracts international attention is Ironman Lanzarote, where athletes have to swim 3.8 km, cycle 180 km round the island and finally run a marathon.

CLIMBING

Adventure Lanzarote (tel. 6 16 81 34 31 | www.adventurelanzarote.com) offers a host of outdoor escapades, e.g. climbing on 650 ft-high rock faces, caving, abseiling and other 'extreme' sports.

CYCLING

The weather on Lanzarote is perfect for all two-wheel enthusiasts. You can safely

On land, on water, on a windsurfing board or a mountain bike: there are plenty of opportunities for action on this small island

leave your waterproof clothing at home. Much more important is a plentiful supply of sunblock and a pair of sunglasses. A light windcheater is recommended for the cooler north and for early mornings and evenings. The hilly north and the magnificent volcanic landscape around Costa Teguise are ideal for mountain bikers. But it is strictly forbidden to leave the (generally very good) trails. Racing cyclists and tourers will find near-perfect conditions throughout the island. But only cyclists with a high level of fitness

should attempt a full circuit of the island. That said, it is in theory possible to reach practically every destination on the island from any place within a day. No mountains are higher than 1975 ft. Cyclists will discover countless natural phenomena and scenic attractions on their travels along the south-east coast. Costa Teguise: *Lanzarote Bikes* hires out excellent mountain bikes and offers INSIDER TIP free delivery of bikes to your holiday hotel *(Avda de las Islas Canarias | CC Las Maretes | 16–22 euros per day, 80–*

110 euros per week | tel. 6 51 09 60 57 | www.lanzarote-bikes.com).

Puerto del Carmen: Several bike hire points: *Renner Bikes (daily 10am–7pm | Centro Comercial Marítimo 25 Alto | mountain bikes from 13 euros per day, racing bikes from 16 euros per day | tel. 928 51 06 12 | www.mountainbike-lanzarote. com).*

DIVING

The underwater fauna off the Canary Islands is interesting and varied. There are also a number of shipwrecks to explore. One of the most memorable dives is INSIDER TIP on the coast near La Mala. Countless sting rays and eagle rays live on the seabed in the clear water. All diving schools request a one-off contribution of 12 euros for the decompression chamber in Arrecife.

Costa Teguise: The *Aquatis Diving Centre Lanzarote* offers dives and lessons (also to children). *Playa de las Cucharas | dive 28 euros, with equipment 40 euros | tel. 928 59 04 07 | www.diving-lanzarote.net*

Playa Blanca: *Courses and dives on of-fer at Rubicon Diving. Marina Rubicón Local 77B | 10 dives 400 euros | tel. 928 34 93 46 | www.rubicondiving.com*

Puerto del Carmen: The Playa de la Barrilla near the old harbour is the starting point for many dives. One popular underwater attraction is the *Catedral*, a 20 m lava bubble in a vertical wall. *Safari Diving | Playa de la Barrilla 4 | beginners' courses 60 euros, scuba diving courses from 300 euros | tel. 928 5119 92 | www. safaridiving.com*

Puerto Calero: *Island Watersports* includes in its programme dives from 35 euros, scuba diving courses from 295 euros. *Marina | tel. 928 5118 80 | www. divelanzarote.com*

GOLF

The hilly 18-hole *Lanzarote Golf* course is situated above Puerto del Carmen. Daily *8am–8pm | access via LZ 505 | Green fee 68 euros | tel. 928 94 50 90 | www.lanzarotegolfresort.com.* The 18-hole *Golf Costa Teguise* is north of the town. Non-members may also play on this par 72 course (handicap required).

The golfing greens, here in Costa Teguise, contrast starkly with the large expanses of black lava

Facilities offered include driving range, putting green and also golf lessons. *Daily 8am–8pm | green fee 68 euros | tel. 928 59 05 12 | www.lanzarote-golf.com.*

HANG GLIDING

The preferred launch-pad for hang gliders is the 1650 ft Montaña Tinasoria near Puerto del Carmen. Further information from *Club Vuelo Libre Lanzarote (Teguise |* mobile *6 29 16 11 43 | www.vuelolibrelan zarote.com).*

Lift-offs are possible from various points on the Risco de Famara and near Mala. But take care. The thermals on Lanzarote can be very strong and unpredictable changes in wind direction are frequent. There have already been many serious accidents, so beginners should only take off under expert supervision.

RIDING

Lanzarote a Caballo is a little out of the way. Horseback rides *(1–2 hours, 40–60 euros)* offered in groups, maximum 20 persons. For children up to the age of 8 years, there are six ponies, ideal for youngsters venturing out on horseback for the first time. Camel rides cost 40 euros per hour. *Carretera Arrecife–Yaiza km 17 | tel. 928 83 00 38 | www.lanzaroteaca ballo.com*

SURFING

Experienced surfers reckon the conditions off Playa de Famara, which sees high, long-breaking waves, rank among the best on the island. But caution is advised. There are some dangerous currents in these parts. *Famara Surf School | El Marinero 39 | Caleta de Famara | courses from 39 euros per day | tel. 928 52 86 76 | www.famarasurf.com*

WALKING

There is so much to explore, particularly in the area around the Parque Nacional de Timanfaya. Guides employed by the *Centro de Visitantes* lead free excursions around the national park. Registration: *Mon–Fri 9am–3pm | tel. 928 84 08 39 (see p. 74) Adventure Lanzarote (see Climbing)* organise guided walks through the Fire Mountains.

WINDSURFING

The best places for windsurfing are Costa Teguise and Puerto del Carmen. There are two windsurfing centres, Club La Santa and Playa de las Cucharas in Costa Teguise. International competitions are staged on the turbulent waters renowned for their capricious currents off the Famara beaches as well as in Costa Teguise.

Costa Teguise: Strong side winds blow on the Playa de las Cucharas. *Windsurf Paradise (Calle la Corvina 8 | tel. 928 34 60 22 | www.windsurflanzarote.com)* operate from a sheltered bay, where beginners and less experienced surfers can learn how to handle the board. The *Windsurfing Club (Calle Las Olas 18 | tel. 928 59 07 31 | www.sportaway-lanzarote.com)* also offers very good facilities. Boards cost from 40 euros per day to hire, beginners' courses from 90 euros. At the *Calima Surf school* in La Caleta by Famara beach, watersports services on offer include the loan of windsurfing boards and windsurfing and surfing lessons, and also lessons in kitesurfing (or kiteboarding), an easy sport to learn in which a small surfboard is propelled across the water by a large kite, to which the rider is harnessed. *Calle Achique 14 | tel. 6 26 91 33 69 | www.calimasurf.com*

TRAVEL WITH KIDS

Younger guests are important guests. There are children's pools and playgrounds in almost all of the holiday complexes.

Family hotels usually offer a full service for children: supervision, animation with games, sports, play, shows and children's discos (enquire when booking). In addition, there will always be high chairs in the restaurants and free cots in the rooms/apartments. One of Lanzarote's five-star hotel showcases itself as being especially child-friendly. The *Hotel Princesa Yaiza (p. 81)* in Playa Blanca has spacious rooms that could almost be described as suites and include a kitchenette. In addition, there is a baby club, a mini club and a junior club for older children. Hotel guests have free access to the 10,000 sq m *Kiko-land (see p. 101)* with bouncy castles and water slides, adventure playground and entertainers dressed as fairy-tale characters. Professional magicians, clowns and acrobats join in and there are themed days to give variety. Your children will quickly find friends of their own age.

Before booking a hotel or apartment, make sure it is within easy reach of the beach, otherwise you may face long walks along busy roads or dusty footpaths. Supermarkets stock all baby requirements, e.g. food, toys, disposable nappies.

The sheltered beaches at Puerto del Carmen and Playa Blanca are perfect for youngsters, as there are no high waves or strong currents. More care is needed in Costa Teguise, because the winds and waves are stronger there. Only Playa del

Photo: On Playa Mujeres

Pools of their own, playgrounds, shows, there's even a children's park: youngsters holidaying on Lanzarote can never get bored

Jablillo is suitable for younger children. Parents should avoid altogether Playa de Famara, because of the choppy inshore waters and unpredictable currents.

For Lanzarotean children, the highlight of Christmas is not Christmas Day but Epiphany (6 January). Like everywhere else in Spain, children receive their Christmas presents on the morning of Reyes Magos. According to tradition, on this day the Three Kings arrived in Bethlehem to deliver their gifts to the baby Jesus. True to the story of the Nativity, on Lanzarote the Three Kings arrive on camels. In some places, such as Arrecife and Yaiza, the day is marked by processions. At carnival time at the start of Lent, children have their own festival and crown their own *reina de carnaval*, the carnival queen.

ARRECIFE

PLAYGROUNDS AND PARTY TIME
Many public facilities and parks provide large sandpits and good play equipment, such as climbing frames, swings and slides.

Everyone needs to soak up the sun after a swim

mini-scooters, playground, sun loungers and a snack bar. However, admission prices are inflated. Children from the age of six will get most from the water park. *Daily 10am–6pm (only open in the summer) | admission for adults 21 euros, children 15 euros, loungers 2.50 euros*

INSIDER TIP LANZAROTE AQUARIUM ●
(125 E4) (*ℳ G 9*)
About 20 well-illuminated tanks re-create the habitats of many sea creatures. The underwater kingdom on show here in all shapes and sizes includes sea cucumbers, spider crabs, clownfish, moray eels and rays. Mussels are bred in lava pools, but the sharks are the main attraction. They can be seen swimming in a glass tunnel directly above the visitors. It is even possible to observe fish embryos growing in the egg. *Daily 10am–6pm | Avda Las Acacias | adults 12 euros, children 8 euros | www.aquariumlanzarote.com*

In Puerto del Carmen *(daily 10am–midnight| CC Biosfera | 4 euros per hour)* and Playa Honda *(daily 10am–10pm| CC Deiland | 4 euros per hour)*, children from 4 to 12 years can play under supervision in playgrounds with a wide range of equipment. Shops in the Dulcipé chain sell nibbles and also INSIDER TIP piñatas, for the party game beloved of Spanish children. Brightly coloured containers are filled with sweets and then broken by the youngsters, spilling their contents on the ground.

TROPICAL PARK (121 D4) (*ℳ G 5*)
Guinate Tropical Bird, Animal & Penguin Park near Guinate in the north covers an area of 11 acres. Birds are the most colourful members of this animal community, with toucans, peacocks and flamingos among the highlights. One memorable feature is the walk-through aviary. Baby birds can be observed in the breeding station and with luck you might even see an egg hatching.

Children are always fond of the shows, which take place several times a day. Parrots that can cycle, count and perform other tricks are the real celebrities here. The labelling of the birds in the aviaries is very sketchy. Other enclosures keep monkeys, meerkats and coatis. Reptiles and fish, including Japanese giant carp, are also popular attractions. The Tropical Park is recommended for families with children from the age of four. *Daily*

COSTA TEGUISE AND THE NORTH

AQUAPARK (125 E4) (*ℳ G 9*)
Apart from hotel pools, the freshwater swimming pool at the golf course in Costa Teguise is the only alternative to the sea. There are a dozen water slides, several pools, paddling pools, trampoline,

10am–5pm | admission for adults 14 euros, children 6 euros | www.guinatepark.com

PUERTO DEL CARMEN AND THE CENTRE

RANCHO TEXAS PARK
(127 F4) (*D 10*)

This former ranch has been expanded to include an adventure and animal park. Among the creatures in the enclosures are turtles, lizards, bison, deer, pumas, armadillos and raccoons. The white tigers attract a lot of attention too. Children love to play in the Sioux village and are thrilled by the performances of the parrots, raptors and sea lions. They can search for gold treasure and go canoeing. Once or twice a week there's a Western night *(Tue, Fri, Sat 7pm–11pm | adults 43 euros, children 25 euros | tel. 928 84 12 86)* with entertainment and barbecue. Shuttle buses operate between the park and holiday resorts. *Daily 9.30am–5.30pm | leave Puerto del Carmen on Calle Noruega and cross under the bypass | adults 15 euros, children (3–12 years) 10 euros | www.ranchotexas lanzarote.com*

TIMANFAYA NATIONAL PARK

DROMEDARIES (122 C5) (*C 9*)

Apart from sun, sand and sea, Lanzarote has few attractions for the younger generation. However, a ride through the fields of black lava in the Timanfaya National Park on a dromedary is an out-of-the-ordinary experience. When children ride with an adult, a bag of sand is attached to their seat. The object is to even out the weight difference between the two riders, so the dromedary is not overloaded on one side. If you specifically ask, smaller children can usually ride on the back of the animal, with parents in seats on the right and left. Youngsters get closer to these hard-working animals at the dromedary station on the edge of Timanfaya National Park. Suitable for children from 3 years. *Daily 9am–4pm (duration approx. 20 minutes) | 12 euros per dromedary*

PLAYA BLANCA

INSIDER TIP KIKOLAND
(126 B6) (*B 12*)

Attractions at this sports and children's playground include several pools, bouncy castle, loungers and lots more. It is suitable for youngsters from 3 years of age under parental supervision. Children's birthday parties organised on request. *Daily 10am–6pm | next to the Hotel Princesa Yaiza | admission for families 24 euros*

A real adventure: riding a dromedary among the volcanoes

FESTIVALS & EVENTS

Nearly all festivals on Lanzarote have a religious origin, be it the veneration of a patron saint or the commemoration of a miracle. The highlight is usually a procession, in which the image of a saint is carried through the streets. There is always be music and dancing. However, doleful tunes and chanting, such as the *folías*, reflect the island's barren land and its isolation. There are compensations: for every festival there is a party, often loud and colourful. Salsa and rock music performed by bands on mobile stages resonates around the alleyways of towns and villages. And everyone joins in – whether aged eight or 80.

Festivals, concerts and theatrical events are staged in the spectacular cave auditorium of *Jameos del Agua* throughout the year. But INSIDER TIP the occasional concerts in the auditorium at the *Cueva de los Verdes* are actually more atmospheric. Information from the tourist office and *www.centrosturisticos.com*

PUBLIC HOLIDAYS

1 Jan: *Año Nuevo*, New Year's Day; **6 Jan:** *Los Reyes*, Epiphany; **19 March:** *San José*, St Joseph's Day; **March/April:** *Viernes Santo*, Good Friday; **1 May:** *Día del Trabajo*, Labour Day; **30 May:** *Día de las Islas Canarias*, Canary Islands Day; **May/June:** *Corpus Christi*; **25 July:** *Santiago Apóstol*, St James' Day; **15 Aug:** *Asunción*, Assumption of the Blessed Virgin; **15 Sept:** *Romería de Mancha Blanca;* **12 Oct:** *Día de la Hispanidad*, Day of the Discovery of America; **1 Nov:** *Todos los Santos*, All Saints Day; **6 Dec:** *Día de la Constitución*, Constitution Day; **8 Dec:** *Inmaculada Concepción*, Immaculate Conception; **25 Dec:** *Navidad*, Christmas

FESTIVALS & EVENTS

6 JANUARY

The Three Kings *(Los Reyes Magos)* ride through Arrecife and other towns and villages on the island, receiving an enthusiastic welcome from the children, who have been waiting excitedly to receive their presents.

FEBRUARY/MARCH

►★ *Carnaval:* The wildest celebration of all starts at the end of January and can go on until early March. Every place has its own dates for the Carnaval festivities and processions. The highlights are the events in Puerto del Carmen, Haría and Arrecife. This riotous and colourful fiesta ends with the ► *entierro de la sardina* or the 'burying of the sardine' ritual.

Festivals on Lanzarote combine religion and folklore. Carnival is always an extravagant celebration

MARCH/APRIL

The processions in Arrecife during the ▶ *Semana Santa* or Holy Week are extravagant celebrations.

MID-MAY

▶ *Feria de Artesanía:* Craft fair in Puerto del Carmen

24 JUNE

▶ INSIDER TIP *Fiesta de San Juan*: Festival to celebrate the harvest and summer solstice, a tradition dating back to the aboriginal settlers. On the eve of the fiesta in Haría, camp-fires are lit and scarecrows burnt.

JULY

▶ *Wine festivals* in Masdache and other places in the vine-growing area of La Geria to music and dancing.

7 JULY

In Femés a week-long festival of special events and processions, the ▶ ★ *Fiesta de San Marcial del Rubicón*, honours the patron saint of Lanzarote.

16 JULY

▶★ *Fiesta de Nuestra Señora del Carmen:* processions are held in Playa Blanca, Puerto del Carmen and La Graciosa to commemorate the patron saint of fishermen.

8 SEPTEMBER

Processions and folklórico events in Yaiza, when the town pays its respects to its saint during the ▶ *Fiesta de la Virgen de los Remedios*.

15 SEPTEMBER

▶ *Romería de Mancha Blanca*: Festival in honour of the Virgen de los Dolores, Our Lady of Sorrows. A statutory public holiday on Lanzarote.

24 DECEMBER

▶★ *Fiesta de los Ranchos de Pascua:* The Christmas party in Teguise is one of the liveliest on the island. First it's processions and prayer, but after midnight the partying starts in earnest with music and dancing. Every year, Yaiza's Belén de Navidad recreates a scene from the Nativity in miniature.

LINKS, BLOGS, APPS & MORE

LINKS

▶ www.panoramio.com A photo-sharing website linked to Google maps. Enter the place you want to visit in the search box and then take a peep at other people's holiday snaps

▶ www.memoriadelanzarote.com This website calls itself the 'island's digital memory'. Text, audio and video clips only available in Spanish, but the countless pictures documenting Lanzarote's history will be of interest to all, even if the language poses problems

▶ www.masscultura.com An easy-to-navigate website mainly in Spanish showcasing forthcoming cultural events in the world of literature, music and art. Click Guia de ocia y cultura Lanzarote for a what's on listing in Spanish and English.

▶ www.outdoorlanzarote.com A collection of mainly medium-length walks on Lanzarote with expert advice and photos

▶ www.lanzaroteinformation.com By far the best source of information about Lanzarote on the web. Everything from where to find the best flight deals to advice on relocating to Lanzarote

BLOGS & FORUMS

▶ www.danistein.com A blog by photographer Dani Stein, who lives on Lanzarote. Do check out this site. You will be amazed by the quality of the photos posted there. He's also on Twitter

▶ www.bloglanzarote. wordpress.com A regularly updated blog with evocative photos

▶ forum.lanzarote.com Another valuable forum for news, events, dates for your diary, articles for sale and views on various topics

Regardless of whether you are still preparing your trip or already in Lanzarote: these addresses will provide you with more information, videos and networks to make your holiday even more enjoyable

▶ www.elviajero.elpais.com/videos/canarias Spain's biggest-circulation daily newspaper contains a variety of videos on the island's most interesting features, e.g. the Timanfaya National Park (in Spanish)

▶ www.lineasromero.com/eng/buceo/safaris.html The website run by the operator of the ferries to the nearby island of La Graciosa has a series of video clips on diving on the island's offshore waters

▶ www.notesinspanish.com Download Spanish lessons to your mp3

▶ www.lanzaroteinformation.com/content/radio-stations-lanzarote There are three English-language stations on Lanzarote, UK Away FM Buzz FM and Holiday FM. Choose your preferred listening from this link. Plus other Spanish stations

▶ www.lanzaroteinformation.com/content/app-qr Use Google Goggles to convert this QR code into an app for your smartphone. Everything you could want to know about Lanzarote while on the move

▶ www.aiexsoftware.com/lanzarote.html Another source of information for your smart phone

▶ Star Walk Lanzarote is the perfect place for stargazing as long as you move away from the main resorts. This app will guide you through the galaxies

▶ The Kite and Windsurfing Navigator Up-to-date forecasts and wind alerts for water sports enthusiasts. Now a free iPhone app

▶ lanzarotetouristnetwork.com Lanzarote information by people who know Lanzarote. A popular site. Need to know more about a hotel or a resort, then someone here will be able to help you.

▶ www.lanzarotegayguide.com and www.gaylanza.com News and information from the island's gay scene. Advice on gay bars, both with forum

TRAVEL TIPS

ARRIVAL

✈ Cheap flights are available from the UK and Ireland with Ryanair, easyjet and Thomas Cook (flight time from UK approx. 4 hours). Flights with no hotel booking cost between 300 and 500 euros. Scheduled flights are much more expensive and nearly always involve a stopover. There are no direct flights from the USA.

The airport near Arrecife on Lanzarote is a drive of between 10 and 30 minutes from the main holiday centres. At busy times there is a direct bus into Arrecife every 30 minutes costing approx. 2 euros. Taxis to Puerto del Carmen cost approx. 12–14 euros, to Costa Teguise 20–24 euros and to Playa Blanca about 40 euros.

🚢 There are ferries leaving from the southern Spanish mainland port of Cádiz every Saturday. The Compañía Trasmediterránea operates a car ferry service, with a crossing taking approx. 32 hours to Arrecife (return Thursday). A single ticket to Lanzarote costs from 280 euros per person (in a 4-bed cabin), a car 262 euros. To book a crossing either visit a travel agency or go online (www.trasmediterranea.es). The same company also operates a ferry service from Cádiz to other Canary Islands and there is an inter-island service. See the website for more information.

BUSES

Scheduled buses (*guaguas*) leave for all the larger villages (but only once or twice a day) from the bus station in Arrecife, the *Estación de Guaguas (Vía Medular | near the stadium | tel. 928 81 15 22)*. All the main tourist centres are served by buses: Puerto del Carmen (no. 2) and Costa Teguise (no. 1) Mon–Fri every 20 minutes, Sat–Sun every 30 minutes, Playa Blanca (no. 6 and 8) Mon–Fri about every hour, Sat and Sun six to eight times a day. Also available for 12 or 22 euros is the *bonobus*, which grants discount fares. *www.arrecifebus.com*

CAMPING

There are no official campsites on the island. 'Wild' camping is not tolerated anywhere.

CAR HIRE

Car hire companies have offices in Arrecife, all the holiday centres and many hotels. To hire a small car costs from approx. 22 euros per day, but expect to pay 260 euros for two weeks (including taxes and fully comprehensive insurance). Off-road

RESPONSIBLE TRAVEL

It doesn't take a lot to be environmentally friendly whilst travelling. Don't just think about your carbon footprint whilst flying to and from your holiday destination but also about how you can protect nature and culture abroad. As a tourist it is especially important to respect nature, look out for local products, cycle instead of driving, save water and much more. If you would like to find out more about eco-tourism please visit: *www.ecotourism.org*

From arrival to weather

From the start to the end of the holiday: useful addresses and information for your trip to Lanzarote

vehicles, motor-cycles (*e.g. from www. felycar.es*) and trikes are considerably more expensive. If you wish to take your hire car on the ferry to Fuerteventura, you must inform the car rental company in advance.

CONSULATES & EMBASSIES

The consulates on Gran Canaria take care of diplomatic and consulate issues for all of the Canary Islands:

UK CONSULATE
Calle Luis Morote 6-3º | Las Palmas de Gran Canaria | tel. 902 109 356 | www. ukinspain.fco.gov.uk

US CONSULATE
Edificio ARCA | C/ Los Martínez Escobar, 3, Oficina 7 | 35007 Las Palmas | tel. 928 27 12 59

CUSTOMS

If you arrive on the Canary Islands from an EU country, no customs checks are necessary. The Canary Islands have a special duty-free tax status and so, as a result, items such as alcohol, tobacco and perfume are considerably cheaper here than on mainland Spain or the rest of Europe. Duty-free allowances for anyone over 17 are as follows: 200 cigarettes or 50 cigars or 250 g tobacco, 50 g of perfume or 250 cl of eau de Cologne, 1 litre of spirits, 2 litres of wine.

EMERGENCY SERVICES

Dial 112 for emergencies of all kinds, e.g. police, fire, ambulance, accident.

HEALTH

It is easy for visitors to misjudge the physical strains that the change in climate places on the body, particularly at the height of summer. If you have a heart condition of any kind, it would probably be safer to visit the island in the winter. Tap water is drinkable, but it is not advisable to consume it in large quantities. All supermarkets sell mineral water in plastic bottles. The European Health Insurance Card (EHIC) entitles citizens of countries in the European Union to free treatment from doctors, who are part of the Spanish Seguridad Social scheme. Travellers from the United States should take out private health insurance. When paying for medical care, ask for a detailed invoice (*factura*), which you can present to your insurance company when you return home.

BUDGETING

Meal	from 7 euros	
	for the dish of the day and a drink in a basic restaurant frequented by locals	
Coffee	from 1 euro	
	for a cortado (espresso with a little milk)	
Beach lounger	5 euros	
	per day	
Wine	from 6 euros	
	for a half-litre carafe of wine	
Petrol	95 cents	
	for one litre of Eurosuper	
Souvenir	from 200 euros	
	for a timple	

SPANISH NATIONAL TOURISM OFFICES

www.spain.info, (*) 00 800 10 10 50 50 – 6th Floor 64 North Row | W1K 7DE London | info.londres@tourspain.es
– 1395 Brickell Avenue, Suite 1130 | Miami, FL 33131 | oetmiami@tourspain.es
– 845 North Michigan Av, Suite 915-E | Chicago, IL 60611 | chicago@tourspain.es
– 8383 Wilshire Blvd., Suite 956 | Beverly Hills, CA 90211 | losangeles@tourspain.es
– 60 East 42nd Street, Suite 5300 (53rd Floor) | New York, NY 10165-0039 | nuevayork@tourspain.es

INFORMATION ON LANZAROTE

PATRONATO DE TURISMO

Brochures, information. *Mon–Fri 9am–3pm | Blas Cabrera Felipe | Arrecife | tel. 928 811762 | www.turismolanzarote. com;* airport information desk open daily. *For further information tel. 928 82 07 04*

PHARMACIES

If you need a pharmacy *(farmacia)* look out for the green cross (usually illuminated) outside. *Opening times: Mon–Fri 9am–13.30pm and 4–8.30 pm, Sat 9am–1pm.* The sign with the words Farmacia de Guardia refers to the nearest pharmacy, which is open for emergencies.

INTERNET

www.abcanarias.com covers all matters of interest to tourists (hotels, hire cars), The tourist board's website *www.turismo lanzarote.com* has up-to-date information on cultural events, beaches, sport, local festivals and similar events.

BOOKS & FILMS

▶ **Mararía** – is a novel written in 1973 by the Spanish writer Rafael Arozarena, subsequently turned into a successful film. The story is about a mysterious woman from Femés called Maria, but who everybody calls Mararia. As a younger woman, she had a chequered love life and then things turned sour. Decades later a stranger arrives in the village and hears her tragic story. It was also made into a film and shot on location in Lanzarote (1998).

▶ **Lanzarote** – is often chosen as a suitable filming location for movies requiring lunar landscapes, the most famous film in this genre one being One Million Years BC (1966). Keen movie enthusiasts, or indeed Raquel Welch fans, will recognise the green lagoon as that of El Golfo. Other films or TV series filmed on Lanzarote include Moby Dick (1956), **When Dinosaurs Ruled the Earth** (1972), **Journey to the Centre of the Earth** (1976), **Doctor Who** (1984), **Enemy Mine** (1986), **The Search for Treasure Island** (1997) and **Broken Embraces** (in Spanish: Los abrazos rotos (2008).

▶ **Lanzarote** – French writer, Michel Houellebecq's short book about Lanzarote (with a volume of his photographs) examines themes around tourism and hedonism.

▶ **Obra Espacial/Arte y Naturaleza** – The Fundación César Manrique sells these two DVDs, which explore the artist's contributions to the island's architecture and art. 25 mins. Both 9 euros.

www.lanzarote.com is a platform for the tourist industry and includes an accommodation search function.

See also p. 104, Links, Blogs, Apps & more

INTERNET CAFÉS

– *Cyberia: Mon–Sat 10am–midnight, Sun 5pm–midnight | Playa Honda | Deiland*
– *Cibercafé Internet: daily 10am–midnight | Puerto del Carmen | Avda. de las Playas 30*
– *Punto Zero: daily 10am–midnight | Costa Teguise | CC Las Cucharas*
– *Internetcafé: daily 10am-midnight | Playa Blanca | promenade near the Restaurant Almacén de la Sal*

MEDIA

There are three English-language stations on Lanzarote, UK Away FM Buzz FM and Holiday FM. English newspapers and magazines are sold in the main holiday centres. See also p. 104, Links, Blogs, Apps & more

Another word: El Golfo

MONEY & CREDIT CARDS

ATMs or cash machines are an inexpensive way to withdraw cash from your account. Check with your bank that you are able to use your card abroad before you leave home and note that cards with PIN numbers longer than 4 digits will not work in Spain. Check also the fees you will be charged for withdrawing foreign currency. Credit cards are accepted in almost all hotels, shops, restaurants and service stations. Bank opening times: *Mon–Fri 8.30am–2pm, Sat 8.30am–1pm*. Some banks open during the afternoon one day a week.

PHONE & MOBILE PHONE

Most telephone boxes take coins and phone cards *(tarjeta telefónica)*. These can be purchased in shops and at newspaper kiosks. A three-minute conversation costs from 2 euros, after 10pm approx. 60 cents.

UK dialling code: 0044
USA dialling code: 001

This is followed by the local area code without the zero and the number you are calling. In the holiday centres, you will find call shops *(locutorio)*, where the caller is billed for the call when it is terminated. The dialling code for Lanzarote is the same as for Spain: 0034 if calling from either the UK or Ireland, 01134 from the USA. Movistar, Vodafone and Orange operate networks for mobile phones on Lanzarote. In 2011 the EU legislated to force the mobile phone companies to reduce roaming charges throughout Europe and so now it makes no difference which network your mobile connects to. Spanish pre-paid cards, such as the Happy Movil, have very low tariffs if you wish to call home. Remember though that you would need to tell any possible callers that you have a new (Spanish) number. These pre-paid cards are available in supermarkets, phone shops and tobacconists. While texts are the cheapest way of communicating with friends and family at home, voicemail messages can entail high costs, so remember to switch this function off before you leave home.

Costa Teguise: the magnificent palm trees create an exotic atmosphere

CURRENCY CONVERTER

£	€	€	£
1	1.10	1	0.90
3	3.30	3	2.70
5	5.50	5	4.50
13	14.30	13	11.70
40	44	40	36
75	82.50	75	67.50
120	132	120	108
250	275	250	225
500	550	500	450

$	€	€	$
1	0.70	1	1.40
3	2.10	3	4.20
5	3.50	5	7
13	9.10	13	18.20
40	28	40	56
75	52.50	75	105
120	84	120	168
250	175	250	350
500	350	500	700

For current exchange rates see www.xe.com

POST

A letter *(carta)* or a postcard *(postal)* to countries within the EU requires a stamp *(sellos)* costing 64 cents.

PRICES

A beer in a bar for the locals is likely to cost around 1.50 euros, a tapa from 3 euros and the dish of the day 5 euros. The same beer will probably cost twice that amount in a bar in one of the holiday centres.

SWIMMING

There are some dangerous currents in the waters off Lanzarote's beaches, so always take heed of the warning flags or notice boards. A red flag means you must not enter the water at all, green indicates safe bathing conditions, yellow means bathe with caution.

TAXI

Taxis on Lanzarote carry a roof sign with a green light and number, plus the letters SP on the number plate. All taxis must be licensed and equipped with a taximeter, which must be switched on before every journey. The basic charge is around 2.30 euros, then 1 euro for every further kilometre. If you hire a taxi to take you on a round-the-island tour, make sure you agree a price beforehand.

TIME

Unlike mainland Spain, Lanzarote runs on Greenwich Mean Time, so visitors from the UK and Ireland do not need to adjust their watches.

WEATHER, WHEN TO GO

The climate on Lanzarote is mild. However, in the summer months it can get oppressively hot, while winter evenings are quite cool because of the constant trade winds. The best times to visit the island are the moderately warm months from November to March. During the holiday months of August and September and around Easter, many mainland Spaniards visit the island.

WEATHER IN ARRECIFE

	Jan	Feb	March	April	May	June	July	Aug	Sept	Oct	Nov	Dec
Daytime temperatures in °C/°F												
	21/70	22/72	23/73	23/73	23/73	25/77	28/82	29/84	29/84	27/81	25/77	20/68
Nighttime temperatures in °C/°F												
	13/55	13/55	14/57	14/57	15/59	16/61	18/64	18/64	18/64	19/66	16/61	14/57
Sunshine hours/day												
	6	7	8	9	9	9	9	9	7	7	6	6
Precipitation days/month												
	3	2	2	1	0	0	0	0	1	1	4	5
Water temperature in °C/°F												
	18/64	18/64	17/63	17/63	18/64	20/68	20/68	21/70	22/72	22/72	20/68	19/66

USEFUL PHRASES SPANISH

PRONUNCIATION

c	before 'e' and 'i' like 'th' in 'thin'
ch	as in English
g	before 'e' and 'i' like the 'ch' in Scottish 'loch'
gue, gui	like 'get', 'give'
que, qui	the 'u' is not spoken, i.e. 'ke', 'ki'
j	always like the 'ch' in Scottish 'loch'
ll	like 'lli' in 'million'; some speak it like 'y' in 'yet'
ñ	'nj'
z	like 'th' in 'thin'

IN BRIEF

Yes/No/Maybe	sí/no/quizás
Please/Thank you	por favor/gracias
Hello!/Goodbye!/See you	¡Hola!/¡Adiós!/¡Hasta luego!
Good morning!/afternoon!/evening!/night!	¡Buenos días!/¡Buenos días!/¡Buenas tardes!/¡Buenas noches!
Excuse me, please!	¡Perdona!/¡Perdone!
May I ...?/Pardon?	¿Puedo ...?/¿Cómo dice?
My name is ...	Me llamo ...
What's your name?	¿Cómo se llama usted?/¿Cómo te llamas?
I'm from ...	Soy de ...
I would like to .../Have you got ...?	Querría .../¿Tiene usted ...?
How much is ...?	¿Cuánto cuesta ...?
I (don't) like that	Esto (no) me gusta.
good/bad/broken/doesn't work	bien/mal/roto/no funciona
too much/much/little/all/nothing	demasiado/mucho/poco/todo/nada
Help!/Attention!/Caution!	¡Socorro!/¡Atención!/¡Cuidado!
ambulance/police/fire brigade	ambulancia/policía/bomberos
May I take a photo here	¿Podría fotografiar aquí?

DATE & TIME

Monday/Tuesday/Wednesday	lunes/martes/miércoles
Thursday/Friday/Saturday	jueves/viernes/sábado
Sunday/working day/holiday	domingo/laborable/festivo
today/tomorrow/yesterday	hoy/mañana/ayer

¿Hablas español?

"Do you speak Spanish?" This guide will help you to say the basic words and phrases in Spanish.

hour/minute/second/moment	hora/minuto/segundo/momento
day/night/week/month/year	día/noche/semana/mes/año
now/immediately/before/after	ahora/enseguida/antes/después
What time is it?	¿Qué hora es?
It's three o'clock/It's half past three	Son las tres/Son las tres y media
a quarter to four/a quarter past four	cuatro menos cuarto/ cuatro y cuarto

TRAVEL

open/closed/opening times	abierto/cerrado/horario
entrance / exit	entrada/acceso salida
departure/arrival	salida/llegada
toilets/ladies/gentlemen	aseos/señoras/caballeros
free/occupied	libre/ocupado
(not) drinking water	agua (no) potable
Where is ...?/Where are ...?	¿Dónde está ...? /¿Dónde están ...?
left/right	izquierda/derecha
straight ahead/back	recto/atrás
close/far	cerca/lejos
traffic lights/corner/crossing	semáforo/esquina/cruce
bus/tram/U-underground/ taxi/cab	autobús/tranvía/metro/ taxi
bus stop/cab stand	parada/parada de taxis
parking lot/parking garage	parking/garaje
street map/map	plano de la ciudad/mapa
train station/harbour/airport	estación/puerto/aeropuerto
ferry/quay	transbordador/muelle
schedule/ticket/supplement	horario/billete/suplemento
single/return	sencillo/ida y vuelta
train/track/platform	tren/vía/andén
delay/strike	retraso/huelga
I would like to rent ...	Querría ... alquilar
a car/a bicycle/a boat	un coche/una bicicleta/un barco
petrol/gas station	gasolinera
petrol/gas / diesel	gasolina/diesel
breakdown/repair shop	avería/taller

FOOD & DRINK

Could you please book a table for tonight for four?	Resérvenos, por favor, una mesa para cuatro personas para hoy por la noche.
on the terrace/by the window	en la terraza/junto a la ventana

The menu, please/	¡El menú, por favor!
Could I please have …?	¿Podría traerme … por favor?
bottle/carafe/glass	botella/jarra/vaso
knife/fork/spoon	cuchillo/tenedor/cuchara
salt/pepper/sugar	sal/pimienta/azúcar
vinegar/oil/milk/cream/lemon	vinagre/aceite/leche/limón
cold/too salty/not cooked	frío/demasiado salado/sin hacer
with/without ice/sparkling	con/sin hielo/gas
vegetarian/allergy	vegetariano/vegetariana/alergía
May I have the bill, please?	Querría pagar, por favor.
bill/receipt/tip	cuenta/recibo/propina

SHOPPING

pharmacy/chemist	farmacia/droguería
baker/market	panadería/mercado
butcher/fishmonger	carnicería/pescadería
shopping centre/department store	centro comercial/grandes almacenes
shop/supermarket/kiosk	tienda/supermercado/quiosco
100 grammes/1 kilo	cien gramos/un kilo
expensive/cheap/price/more/less	caro/barato/precio/más/menos
organically grown	de cultivo ecológico

ACCOMMODATION

I have booked a room	He reservado una habitación.
Do you have any … left?	¿Tiene todavía …?
single room/double room	habitación individual/habitación doble
breakfast/half board/	desayuno/media pensión/
full board (American plan)	pensión completa
at the front/seafront/garden view	hacia delante/hacia el mar/hacia el jardín
shower/sit-down bath	ducha/baño
balcony/terrace	balcón/terraza
key/room card	llave/tarjeta
luggage/suitcase/bag	equipaje/maleta/bolso
swimming pool/spa/sauna	piscina/spa/sauna
soap/toilet paper/nappy (diaper)	jabón/papel higiénico/pañal
cot/high chair/nappy changing	cuna/trona/cambiar los pañales
deposit	anticipo/caución

BANKS, MONEY & CREDIT CARDS

bank/ATM/	banco/cajero automático/
pin code	número secreto
cash/credit card	en efectivo/tarjeta de crédito
bill/coin/change	billete/moneda/cambio

HEALTH

doctor/dentist/paediatrician	médico/dentista/pediatra
hospital/emergency clinic	hospital/urgencias
fever/pain/inflamed/injured	fiebre/dolor/inflamado/herido
diarrhoea/nausea/sunburn	diarrea/náusea/quemadura de sol
plaster/bandage/ointment/cream	tirita/vendaje/pomada/crema
pain reliever/tablet/suppository	calmante/comprimido/supositorio

POST, TELECOMMUNICATIONS & MEDIA

stamp/letter/postcard	sello/carta/postal
I need a landline phone card/	Necesito una tarjeta telefónica/
I'm looking for a prepaid card for my mobile	Busco una tarjeta prepago para mi móvil
Where can I find internet access?	¿Dónde encuentro un acceso a internet?
dial/connection/engaged	marcar/conexión/ocupado
socket/adapter/charger	enchufe/adaptador/cargador
computer/battery/ rechargeable battery	ordenador/batería/ batería recargable
e-mail address/at sign (@)	(dirección de) correo electrónico/arroba
internet address (URL)	dirección de internet
internet connection/wifi	conexión a internet/wifi
e-mail/file/print	archivo/imprimir

LEISURE, SPORTS & BEACH

beach/sunshade/lounger	playa/sombrilla/tumbona
low tide/high tide/current	marea baja/marea alta/corriente

NUMBERS

0	cero	14	catorce
1	un, uno, una	15	quince
2	dos	16	dieciséis
3	tres	17	diecisiete
4	cuatro	18	dieciocho
5	cinco	19	diecinueve
6	seis	20	veinte
7	siete	100	cien, ciento
8	ocho	200	doscientos, doscientas
9	nueve	1000	mil
10	diez	2000	dos mil
11	once	10 000	diez mil
12	doce	1/2	medio
13	trece	1/4	un cuarto

NOTES

MARCO POLO TRAVEL GUIDES

MARCO POLO
With ROAD ATLAS & PULL-OUT MAP
LAKE GARDA
E BALDO WITH MOUNTAIN BIKE
ar in Malcesine takes bikes too
SSES" IN SALÒ
ocolate ...bacetti
Travel with Insider Tips

MARCO POLO
With STREET ATLAS & PULL-OUT MAP
NEW YORK
OWS, WILD FLOWERS AND SKYSCRAPERS
chic: the High Line in Chelsea
AIL ON CLOUD NINE
op bar at 230 Fifth Street
Travel with Insider Tips

MARCO POLO
With ROAD ATLAS & PULL-OUT MAP
FRENCH RIVIERA
NICE, CANNES & MONACO
SPECTACULAR GRAND CANYON DU VERDON
Breath-taking scenery that takes some beating
SNIFFING THE AIR
The perfume manufacturers of Grasse
Travel with Insider Tips
www.marcopolouk.com

MARCO POLO
With ROAD ATLAS & PULL-OUT MAP
ALLORCA
AN FLAIR IN THE MEDITERRANEAN
Mallorca's most beautiful beach
VE ...IN" CROWD MEET
Fonda in Deià
Travel with Insider Tips

MARCO POLO
With STREET ATLAS & PULL-OUT MAP
BERLIN
A STUNNING ISLAND JUST FOR ART
Showcasing treasures from around the world
STAY COOL AT NIGHT
scene sets the trend
Travel with Insider Tips

- PACKED WITH INSIDER TIPS
- BEST WALKS AND TOURS
- FULL-COLOUR PULL-OUT MAP
  AND STREET ATLAS

ROAD ATLAS

The green line ___ indicates the Trips & tours (p. 88–93)
The blue line ___ indicates the Perfect route (p. 30–31)

All tours are also marked on the pull-out map

Photo: Haría

Exploring Lanzarote

The map on the back cover shows how the area has been sub-divided

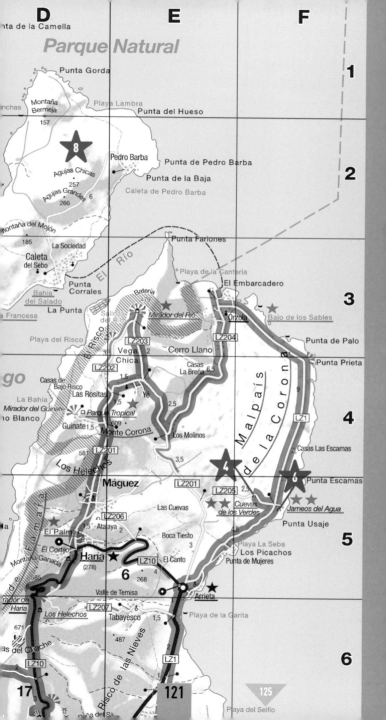

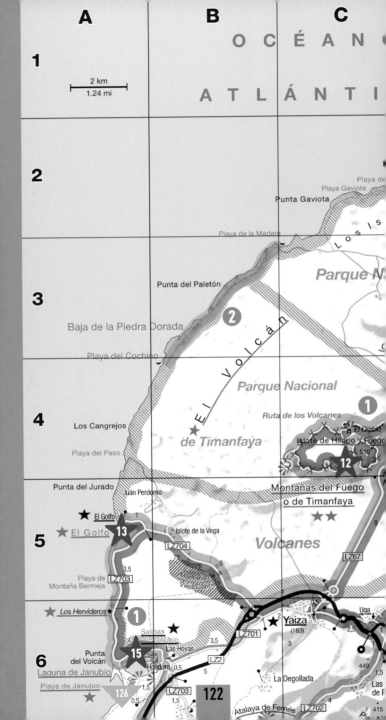

OCÉAN

ATLÁNTI

1

2 km
1.24 mi

2

Playa de
Playa Gaviota
Punta Gaviota

Playa de la Madera

Los Is

3

Punta del Paletón

Baja de la Piedra Dorada

Playa del Cochino

Parque N

2

El Volcán

4

Los Cangrejos

Playa del Paso

★ de Timanfaya

Parque Nacional

Ruta de los Volcanes

1

El Diablo

Islote de Hilario Fuego

510

★ **12**

5

Punta del Jurado

Juan Perdomo

★ El Golfo

★ El Golfo **13**

Islote de la Vega

LZ704

226

Montaña de
Vieja Gabino

Playa de
Montaña Bermeja LZ703

3,5

Montañas del Fuego
o de Timanfaya

★★

Volcanes

LZ67

8

6

★ Los Hervideros ★ **1**

Punta
del Volcán

Laguna de Janubio

Playa de Janubio ★

★ **15**

Salinas
de Janubio

La
Hondura

Las Hoyas

126

0,5

0,5

1,5

LZ703

1,5

3,5

LZ2

5

5

★ Yaiza
(183)

LZ701

3

La Degollada

Atalaya de Femés LZ702

122

Uga

2,5

449

1,5

Las
de F

415

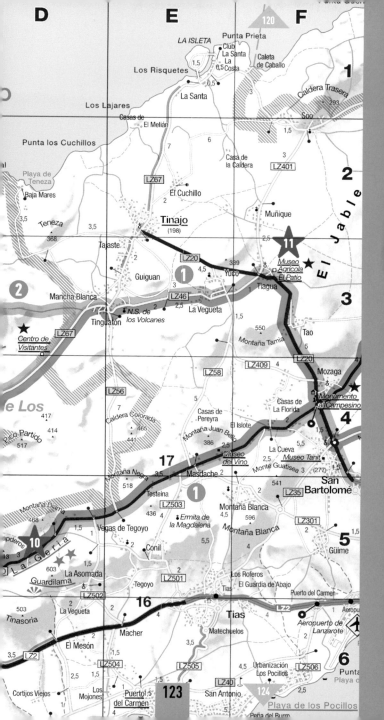

D   E   F

Punta Gach...

120

LA ISLETA   Punta Prieta

Club
La Santa
La 0,5
Costa

Caleta
de Caballo

1

Los Risquetes

0,5

Caldera Trasera

La Santa

Los Lajares

293

Soo

Casas de
El Melián

1,5

Punta los Cuchillos

6

Casa de
la Caldera

LZ401

2

Playa de
Teneza

LZ67

7

Baja Mares

El Cuchillo

Muñique

3,5

Teneza

2

368

3,5

Tinajo
(198)

389

Museo
Agrícola
El Patio ★

11

El Jable

Tajaste

LZ20

2,5

Guiguan

1

4,5

Yuco

3

Tiagua

2

Mancha Blanca

LZ46

2,5

La Vegueta

550

Tao

Tinguatón

N.S. de
los Volcanes

1,5

2

Montaña Tamia

5

Centro de
Visitantes

LZ67

LZ20

e Los

LZ58

LZ409

Mozaga

Monumento
al Campesino ★

4

417

LZ56

5

Casas de
La Florida

Pico Partido

414

7

Caldera Colorada

465

Casas de
Pereyra

2

El Islote

517

441

Montaña Juan Bello

386

La Cueva

5,5

Museo Tanit

Montaña Negra

17

Museo
del Vino

2,5

Monte Guatisea 3

(277)

518

3,5

Masdache

541

San
Bartolomé

apderos

Montaña Diama

Testeina

LZ503

1

LZ35

10

468

436

4

Ermita de
la Magdalena

Montaña Blanca

4,5

596

LZ301

La Gleria

1,5

Vegas de Tegoyo

Montaña Blanca

5

Güime

603

La Asomada

1,5

2

Conil

5,5

4

Guardilama

LZ501

Tegoyo

Los Roferos

503

LZ502

16

El Guardia de Abajo

Puerto del Carmen

Tinasoria

La Vegueta

Tias

Tias

1

Aeropu

El Mesón

Macher

3,5

Aeropuerto de
Lanzarote

3,5

LZ2

Matechuelos

LZ504

1,5

LZ505

4,5

Urbanización
Los Pocillos

LZ506

6

Cortijos Viejos

Los
Mojones

1,5

Puerto
del Carmen

123

San Antonio

LZ40

124

2,5

Punta

Playa d

Peña del Burr...

Playa de los Pocillos

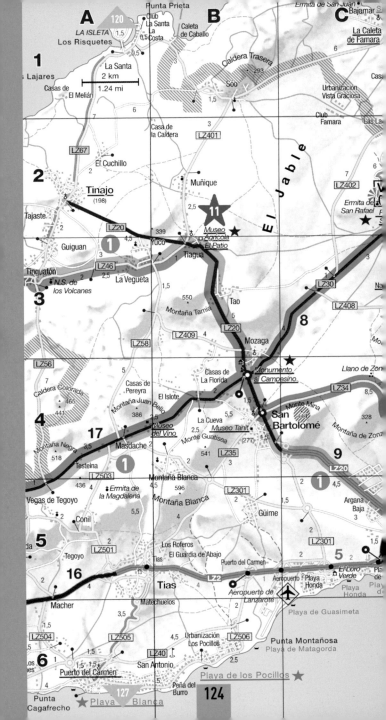

D **E** **F**

Playa Camara

Risco de Famara

Los Helechos · Tabayesco · Playa de la Garita

121

671 · Peñas del Chache

487

1

Urbanización · nara · Ermita de las Nieves · **17** · LZ10

LZ1

El Cangrejo

1,5

Mala · Playa del Seifío

Peña del Silvo · 394 · Los Arrabales

Parque Eólico · Los Valles · Ermita

4,5 · **5** · Museo · 3

Risco de las Nieves

2

Charco del Palo

Jardín de Cactus · Guatiza · Urb. ANAC

Ermita de San José

2,5 · 1,5 · 4 · LZ406

3,5 · Ermita de San Sebastián · El Mojón

Cast. de Santa Barbara · (260)

1,5 · **19** · 1,5 · 323 · 8,5 · Urbanización Los Cocoteros

LZ404 · Tinamala

Teguise · 2 · napay · 1,5 · 2,5

Teseguite · LZ1

Playa del Tío Joaquin

3

Urbanización Oasis de Nazaret

Las Honduras

Las Mesetas

Urbanización Las Cabreras · 3 · 235

Montaña Corona · Punta de Tierra Negra

321 · Tahiche

3 · El Rostro

6 · Punta de la Corvina

8 · El Charco

4

Playa de las Cucharas

LZ1 · **4** · Costa Teguise · Punta de Tope

ados · 2 · 4 · Playa Bastián

olcán de Tahiche · LZ14 · Las Caletas

1,5 · 1,5 · Punta de Lomo Gordo

1 · 1,5 · 1,5

3 · Punta Grande

1,5 · Playa de la Arena

Cast. de San José

Cádiz

ISLA DE CRUCES

5

ISLA DEL FRANCES · Cast. de San Gabriel

RMINA · Punta de la Lagarta

ecife

O C É A N O

3

A T L Á N T I C O

6

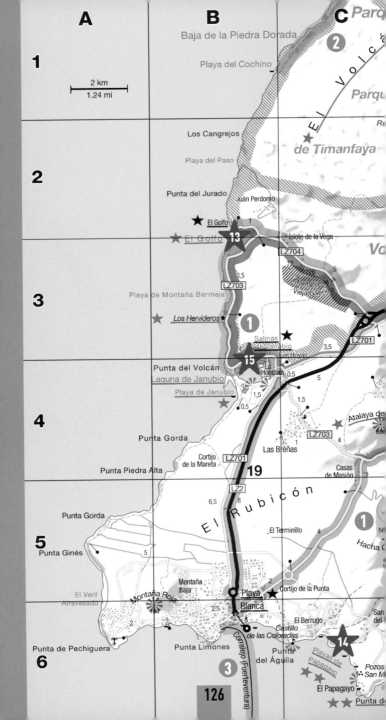

	A	B	C

1

Baja de la Piedra Dorada

Playa del Cochino

2 km
1.24 mi

Parq

El Vol

2

Los Cangrejos

Playa del Paso

Parqu

de Timanfaya

Punta del Jurado

Juan Perdomo

★ El Golfo

13

★ El Golfo

Islote de la Vega

LZ704

Vo

3

Playa de Montaña Bermeja

3,5

LZ703

Montaña de la
Vieja/Gabriela

★ Los Hervideros ★

1

Salinas
de Janubio

★

LZ701

Punta del Volcán

15

Las Hoyas

3,5

4

Laguna de Janubio

La
Honduña 0,5

Playa de Janubio

5

0,5

1,5

1,5

Atalaya de

Punta Gorda

LZ703

4

Punta Piedra Alta

Cortijo
de la Mareta

LZ701

Las Breñas

Casas
de Masión

19

LZ2

El Rubicón

6,5 8

5

Punta Gorda

El Terminillo

4

1

Punta Ginés

5

Hacha

Montaña
Baja

El Veril
Atravesado

Montaña Roja

2

Playa
Blanca

Cortijo de la Punta

★

El Berrugo

San
del

2,5

Castillo
de las Coloradas

14
★

Punta de Pechiguera

Punta Limones

Punta
del Águila

Playa de
Papagayo

Pozos
San M

6

3

El Papagayo

★★

★★ Punta de

126

Corralejo (Fuerteventura)

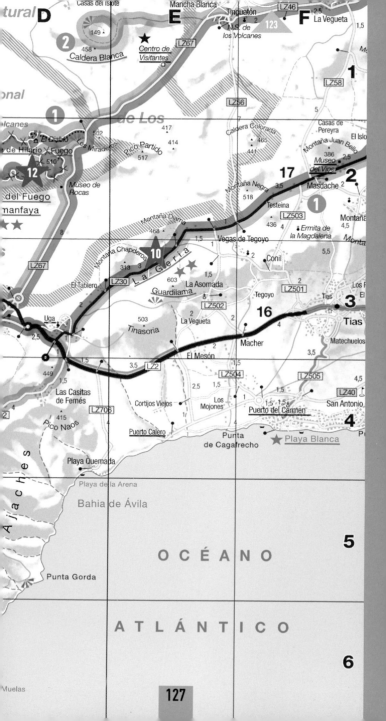

KEY TO ROAD ATLAS

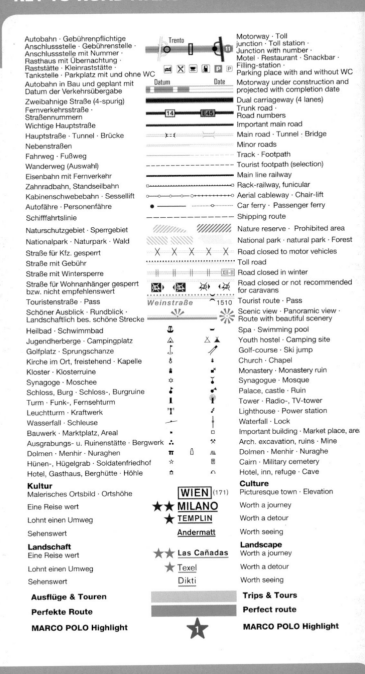

Autobahn · Gebührenpflichtige Anschlussstelle · Gebührenstelle · Anschlussstelle mit Nummer · Rasthaus mit Übernachtung · Raststätte · Kleinraststätte · Tankstelle · Parkplatz mit und ohne WC	Trento	Motorway · Toll junction · Toll station · Junction with number · Motel · Restaurant · Snackbar · Filling-station · Parking place with and without WC
Autobahn in Bau und geplant mit Datum der Verkehrsübergabe	Datum / Date	Motorway under construction and projected with completion date
Zweibahnige Straße (4-spurig)		Dual carriageway (4 lanes)
Fernverkehrsstraße · Straßennummern	14 / E45	Trunk road · Road numbers
Wichtige Hauptstraße		Important main road
Hauptstraße · Tunnel · Brücke		Main road · Tunnel · Bridge
Nebenstraßen		Minor roads
Fahrweg · Fußweg		Track · Footpath
Wanderweg (Auswahl)		Tourist footpath (selection)
Eisenbahn mit Fernverkehr		Main line railway
Zahnradbahn, Standseilbahn		Rack-railway, funicular
Kabinenschwebebahn · Sessellift		Aerial cableway · Chair-lift
Autofähre · Personenfähre		Car ferry · Passenger ferry
Schifffahrtslinie		Shipping route
Naturschutzgebiet · Sperrgebiet		Nature reserve · Prohibited area
Nationalpark · Naturpark · Wald		National park · natural park · Forest
Straße für Kfz. gesperrt	X X X X X	Road closed to motor vehicles
Straße mit Gebühr		Toll road
Straße mit Wintersperre	XII-II	Road closed in winter
Straße für Wohnanhänger gesperrt bzw. nicht empfehlenswert		Road closed or not recommended for caravans
Touristenstraße · Pass	Weinstraße · ^1510	Tourist route · Pass
Schöner Ausblick · Rundblick · Landschaftlich bes. schöne Strecke		Scenic view · Panoramic view · Route with beautiful scenery
Heilbad · Schwimmbad		Spa · Swimming pool
Jugendherberge · Campingplatz	△ / X △	Youth hostel · Camping site
Golfplatz · Sprungschanze		Golf-course · Ski jump
Kirche im Ort, freistehend · Kapelle		Church · Chapel
Kloster · Klosterruine		Monastery · Monastery ruin
Synagoge · Moschee		Synagogue · Mosque
Schloss, Burg · Schloss-, Burgruine		Palace, castle · Ruin
Turm · Funk-, Fernsehturm		Tower · Radio-, TV-tower
Leuchtturm · Kraftwerk		Lighthouse · Power station
Wasserfall · Schleuse		Waterfall · Lock
Bauwerk · Marktplatz, Areal		Important building · Market place, are
Ausgrabungs- u. Ruinenstätte · Bergwerk		Arch. excavation, ruins · Mine
Dolmen · Menhir · Nuraghen	π / 0 / ⏛	Dolmen · Menhir · Nuraghe
Hünen-, Hügelgrab · Soldatenfriedhof	☆ / ⊞	Cairn · Military cemetery
Hotel, Gasthaus, Berghütte · Höhle	⌂ / ∩	Hotel, inn, refuge · Cave

Kultur		**Culture**
Malerisches Ortsbild · Ortshöhe	WIEN (171)	Picturesque town · Elevation
Eine Reise wert	★★ MILANO	Worth a journey
Lohnt einen Umweg	★ TEMPLIN	Worth a detour
Sehenswert	Andermatt	Worth seeing

Landschaft		**Landscape**
Eine Reise wert	★★ Las Cañadas	Worth a journey
Lohnt einen Umweg	★ Texel	Worth a detour
Sehenswert	Dikti	Worth seeing

Ausflüge & Touren		**Trips & Tours**
Perfekte Route		**Perfect route**
MARCO POLO Highlight	★ 1	**MARCO POLO Highlight**

DOS & DON'TS

A few things to bear in mind on Lanzarote

DON'T FALL FOR COUNTERFEITS

Only buy watches and branded clothing in large stores. Any bargains you find in bazaars and flea markets are counterfeits. The same applies to 'genuine Canarian' products. Ivory elephants and other African carvings are painted hardwood.

DON'T FRY IN THE WINTER SUN

The main health risk on Lanzarote is the high level of solar radiation, even in the winter. Fair-skinned northern Europeans often underestimate the power of the winter sun. A sunblock with a high sun-protection factor is essential. Children should keep bare skin covered. Some sort of hat, which will also protect the neck, is also important.

DON'T PAY SEPARATELY

If you are dining in a restaurant or drinking in a bar and then ask to pay separately when settling the bill, you are likely to get an unsympathetic response from Canary Islanders.

DON'T GET LURED ON TO A PROMOTIONAL BUS TOUR

Free island sightseeing tours, with coffee and cakes included, are used to hard sell poor-quality goods. In the end, the normal coach tours turn out to be cheaper.

DON'T SHOW TOO MUCH BARE FLESH

For men to wander through the streets semi-naked or to sit in a café bare-chested is to show contempt for Canarian customs.

DON'T BELIEVE WHAT THE TIME-SHARE SELLERS SAY

The dream: a second home on Lanzarote. The idea: paying for time. You receive a share in a property and residence rights for a specific time of the year. But do take care. This version of a carefree holiday only pays off for the seller. Before you know it, this overpriced apartment will become a drain on your finances.

DON'T PAY TOO MUCH FOR THE INTERNET IN HOTELS

Many hotels offer their guests internet access or WiFi. But the cost of surfing the worldwide web quickly mounts up. Complain at hotel reception. Nowadays this service should be free everywhere.

DON'T BUY CHEAP ELECTRONIC GOODS

Rogue traders in camcorders, digital cameras, etc. (Playa Blanca is notorious) peddle overpriced junk as bargains and, on top of that, there is a risk of fraud if paying by credit card. As a general rule pay/sign only after you have the goods in your hands.

WRITE TO US

e-mail: info@marcopologuides.co.uk

Did you have a great holiday?
Is there something on your mind?
Whatever it is, let us know!
Whether you want to praise, alert us
to errors or give us a personal tip –
MARCO POLO would be pleased to
hear from you.
We do everything we can to provide
the very latest information for your trip.

Nevertheless, despite all of our authors'
thorough research, errors can creep
in. MARCO POLO does not accept any
liability for this. Please contact us by
e-mail or post.

MARCO POLO Travel Publishing Ltd
Pinewood, Chineham Business Park
Crockford Lane, Chineham
Basingstoke, Hampshire RG24 8AL
United Kingdom

PICTURE CREDITS
Cover photo: Jardin de Cactus, cacti and windmill (Getty Images/Robert Harding World Imagery: Simoni)
Photos: O. Baumli (107); DuMont Bildarchiv: Lumma (29, 87), Widmann (2 centre top, 7, 26 left, 75, 111); © fotolia.
com: lunamarina (17 top); R. Freyer (2 centre, 15, 28/29, 32/33, 37, 38/39, 45, 46, 54, 102/103, 103, 112); I.
Gawin (1 bottom, 58); Getty Images/Robert Harding World Imagery: Simoni (1 top); Hotel Hesperia Lanzarote
(16 bottom); Huber: Ripani (10/11, 106 top), Schmid (2 top, 5), Stadler (27); K. Kallabis (47); R. Jung (53); centre
Kettel (64, 66, 70); Laif: Amme (98/99); Lanzarote Retreats: Ronn Ballantyne (16 top, 16 centre); Look: age foto-
stock (30 right, 90, 93), The Travel Library (30 left, 118/119); mauritius images: AGE (50/51), Alamy (right flap, 6,
62, 94/95, 100, 106 bottom), CuboImages (59, 88/89), imagebroker: Siepmann (9), imagebroker/White Star:
Gumm (8), Layer (20); Moda Indigo S.L. (17 bottom); D. Renckhoff (78, 102); Schapowalow: Nebe (left flap); W.
Taschner (21); M. Thomas (22); White Star: Schiefer (3 bottom, 60/61, 76/77, 81); T. P. Widmann (2 bottom, 3
centre, 4, 12/13, 18/19, 24/25, 26 right, 28, 34, 40/41, 48, 56, 71, 72/73, 82/83, 84, 101); E. Wrba (42, 69, 96);

1st Edition 2012
Worldwide Distribution: Marco Polo Travel Publishing Ltd, Pinewood, Chineham Business Park, Crockford Lane,
Basingstoke, Hampshire RG24 8AL, United Kingdom. Email: sales@marcopolouk.com
© MAIRDUMONT GmbH & Co. KG, Ostfildern
Chief editors: Michaela Lienemann (concept, managing editor), Marion Zorn (concept, text editor)
Author: Sven Weniger; co-author: Izabella Gawin; editor: Jens Bey
Programme supervision: Ann-Katrin Kutzner, Nikolai Michaelis, Silwen Randebrock
Picture editor: Gabriele Forst
What's hot: wunder media, Munich
Cartography road atlas: © MAIRDUMONT, Ostfildern; Cartography pull-out map: © MAIRDUMONT, Ostfildern
Design: milchhof : atelier, Berlin; Front cover, pull-out map cover, page 1: factor product munich
Translated from German by Paul Fletcher, Suffolk; editor of the English edition: John Sykes, Cologne
Phrase book in cooperation with Ernst Klett Sprachen GmbH, Stuttgart, Editorial by Pons Wörterbücher

INDEX

This index lists all sights, museums and destinations plus the names of important people featured in this guide. Numbers in bold indicate a main entry